Meth Survivor- Jennifer's Story

And how one community fought back

Betty Brady

Bloomington, IN   Milton Keynes, UK

authorHOUSE

AuthorHouse™
1663 Liberty Drive, Suite 200
Bloomington, IN 47403
www.authorhouse.com
Phone: 1-800-839-8640

AuthorHouse™ UK Ltd.
500 Avebury Boulevard
Central Milton Keynes, MK9 2BE
www.authorhouse.co.uk
Phone: 08001974150

First published by AuthorHouse 2/10/2006

ISBN: 1-4259-1234-6 (sc)

Printed in the United States of America
Bloomington, Indiana

This book is printed on acid-free paper.

Cover Credit: Don Groce, from Summerville, GA

Dedication

This book is dedicated to all mothers of meth victims. To any mother who has prayed fervently, pleading for the life of her wayward child, or driven the roads seeking that child.

My heart goes out to you. My cry is 'don't give up.' You might be the only lifeline your son or daughter has. There is hope............... don't give up.

If you taught your child right from wrong while they were growing up, that knowledge is still there. Underlying, perhaps, but still there.

God doesn't give up on us that easily, and, by that same token, we can't give up either. Don't give up.

Foreword

This book is being written because of my driving desire to 'touch' others who are or have been struggling with meth. I feel your pain. I've put off this work because I dreaded 'reliving' the nightmare, but I realize we all share pain. No one is an island, and we're all part of the family of man.

I've seen so many 'meth' faces, and so many wrecked lives. So many displaced and neglected children. So much personal and parental responsibility being shifted to the states because someone couldn't or wouldn't do their job. They couldn't because meth had become their priority.

I recall the face of a mother, a former friend of mine, once vibrant and so full of life. She buried her son due to meth, and a year later she was still like a zombie. She needed help just maneuvering aisles at Wal Mart. Grief and painful reality had taken such a toll on her. It's heartbreaking.

The success stories are much better, and the ones I love most. One young mother gave up meth and came home when her youngest of four children found out her location and called her, tearfully pleading. "It doesn't matter if we have nothing to eat, Mama, just please come home." Love for her child won this fight. She came home.

Another woman proudly showed off the fifty pounds she had packed on after a year off meth. She jokingly called herself a 'clean, happy, fat woman.'

We'll take fat over meth any day. Any day.

Our goal is to stress that there is hope. Our communities can fight back. Individuals can come back to sanity and clean living. In fact, many strong recovered users, including my daughter, have a big sense of pride in accomplishment. Whether it's buying or renting their own home, going back to school, or just holding down a job, there is pride and self esteem in recovery. Pride beats a defeated demeanor any day.

Yes !!! Oh, yes ....

Acknowledgements

These are the people who made this effort possible. They are my motivators, my inspiration. Without them, this probably would not have happened.

Kay Thomas - She deserves a medal for all her sacrifices, and personal pain she's endured. Always giving and supportive, Kay's strength is 'like a rock' and a big one at that.

Summerville Police Chief Stan Mosley - A big man with a heart of gold. I've called on Stan so many times, for help, guidance, advice, etc. He's always been there for me. Stan is a true friend, a real gem of a guy.

Ga. Senator Jeff Mullis - An all around great guy, and I'm honored to claim him as my friend. Working tirelessly on the legislative end, Jeff and his constituents were willing to listen to we, the people, and put our needs into action.

Investigator Jesse Hambrick, Jr. - from Douglasville, Ga. Jesse criss crosses the state to offer help and guidance to hard hit communities. He rallies people to the fight against meth and stresses strength in numbers. Jesse inspired our citizen's meth task force, and he's a true credit to his profession.

Vaneta Hullander - from Catoosa County -- to know Vaneta is to be taken aback by her drive, calm demeanor, and dedication to her cause. An accomplished woman, and champ of a lady, she encouraged me to write this book.

Summerville Police Department Resource Officer Clint Young - former core, now advisory member on our task force. To know Clint is to love him. Always helping, always leading, this little man is all heart, and a kid at heart. It's no wonder kids love him so much.

Don Groce - Quiet, very smart, stedfast in all respects. Chemist, singer, family man ... and at all times, first and foremost, obedient to his Lord.

Tommy Pledger - minister of Alpine Church, and one of the friends I called on, requesting prayer for Jennifer. Tommy had his whole congregation pray for her and a week later, she came home. Need I say more? Thank you, Tommy. Thank you, Alpine Church.

Vickie Selman - Core committee member of our Task Force. Always a bundle of positive energy and always on the job.

Other members I'd like to mention are Barbara Griffitt, Remona Wright, Shelia Shelley, and LaRita Burke. These dedicated ladies are amazingly resourceful, full of bright ideas, and all have the stamina to 'git' er done.'

The Summerville News - Chattooga County's legal instrument and bearer of all local news, good and bad. Editor Gene Espy generously allowed us to use all printed materials pertaining to Jennifer and Chattooga's Meth plight. Their coverage has been invaluable toward public awareness.

Last but not least, I think the good people of Chattooga County who are as sick of meth as I am, and willing to take a stand against it, deserve mention. After all, anybody can sit back and gripe. Movers and shakers do something constructive.

God bless all of you good people.

Special
Acknowledgements

We particularly wish to thank our media sources for the tremendous effort toward community awareness which most of them have conducted.

We especially want to thank the following media sources for allowing us to use some of their related articles in this publication.

The Summerville News   ----   from Summerville, GA.
The Rome News Tribune   ----   from Rome, GA.
Walker County Messenger   ----   from Lafayette, GA.
Catoosa County News   ----   from Ringold, GA.
Chattooga Press   ----   from Rome, GA.

and Fairway Outdoor Advertising.

Thank you all very much.

Introduction

June 2003 is the month Jennifer came home from her two to 3 year bout with almost daily methamphetamine. Looking gaunt and sickly, her 5'7" frame was only carrying about 95 pounds. Often, young females dream of being shamelessly slim, but meth had expidited that process and brought many other miseries along with it.

Prior to this, she had been a photographer's dream, beautifully tall and picturesque, with gorgeous black hair and striking blue eyes. Jennifer had definitely been a product of her Irish and Cherokee Indian heritage.

And there she stood, tearfully telling me she was through with meth and wanted to come home and get clean. She handed her car keys to me and said, " No matter what I say or do, don't give these back to me." She proceeded to tell me she was safe at home. Through misty eyes, she apologized for her erratic behavior. "Mom, I'm sorry. I know I've put you through hell. You've always been there for me, and I need you to help me now.

I want my life back. Mom, I'm so tired of dope."

My heart felt like it might explode as I hugged my only daughter. Part of me was thinking, "Is she for real, or are we in for another letdown?" Still, she was home, and stressing her desire to do better. Time would tell if she was really sincere. At least she was home right now.

Over the next few weeks, I saw more maturity and determination in her than I'd ever seen before. Quitting cold turkey had to be both mentally and physically shocking, and she was very sick as a result. Time and time again, nightmares and cold sweats told her story. I would hear her thrashing in bed and go to check on her. Sweat would be rolling. Wild eyed and with heart racing, she was convinced she had done the drug again. She'd say, "Mom, I'm sorry. I slipped up." Actually, she'd never left the room, and no one had entered. Thirty days off the drug and we were learning more and more about the evil of meth. It was still working on her mind, still clinging to her, not wanting to give up it's vicious claim on her. What a monster !!

As the weeks passed, the healing process began and gradually her sleep patterns, appetite and skin color improved noticeably. Still, it took a good eight months of home recovery, completely separated from her old pals, for Jennifer to recover to the point of near normalcy, though she has changed permanently by this experience.

Today, we try to help others who face the hell of the devil drug methamphetamine. Sometimes together, sometimes separate, and the range is from recovery testimony to meth task force projects such as raising public awareness, drug education, promoting drug court, and generally trying to help the ones we can.

This is our story, and I thank God everyday because she's alive and we're able to tell it. Others weren't so fortunate.

Table of Contents

Section One

My Story -- by Jennifer Brady

I am a 26 year old female named Jennifer and this is my story ..... I was a generally happy child. I played outside with my brother and all the neighborhood kids, like most children do. I visited with cousins and other family members. I enjoyed being outdoors for the most part. I recall going fishing with my dad and uncles quite often. I really enjoyed this.

As I got older and into school, I think I had a problem socializing with other kids. I didn't have very many friends. In the 3rd grade, I met my best friend, Kelli. We seemed to have a lot in common and we had a chemistry between the two of us that was irreplaceable. She and I remain friends today.

I was about 12 years old when I had a four wheeler accident that left me with a mild concussion which resulted in a life long problem known as epilepsy. At about 14, the doctor had put me on medicine that controlled my seizures. This problem made me feel a little more distant from other kids my age.

My mother enrolled me in a modeling school. I learned a lot about how to present myself, carrying myself, manners, things like this. I was still very uncomfortable with myself for some reason. I remained unsociable. I did have a wonderful time, though. We

3

would go to conventions where I modeled runway, swimsuit, and photography. I loved it. The attention I received was outstanding. This did help me to realize I had been blessed with a beautiful face, but I remained uncomfortable with the person I was inside.

While in modeling, visiting other states and going to these conventions, I began dabbling with different types of drugs. Mostly alcohol, pot and different pills. At this point, I felt fine. I could do without drugs while I was home with my family. When I hit the streets with my few friends I had, we did all the drugs we could get our hands on. Never realizing or even caring that I was headed down the wrong road. As I began doing more and more drugs, I found a world of friends and people just like me that I felt I could relate to. I still saw Kelli through the years. We remained the best of friends. She was the only friend I felt comfortable with without drugs.

One occasion I remember well when I was only 15 years old, myself and a friend of mine who is now passed went through a local drive-thru window at a fast food restaurant to buy a joint from a guy who worked the window. I wasn't very knowledgeable about different drugs at this point. Little did I know the joint was laced with PCP. I recall feeling really weird compared to my recent highs. The lights had streamers coming off them. Everything seemed to look a lot different than normal. My curfew was 10 p.m. so I made it home and felt as though I couldn't walk. I remember how I felt as I approached the stairs in my parents home. I thought "Oh, no, I will never make it up these damn stairs" so I began to crawl up the steps leading to my bedroom. I remember my parents asking me if I was drunk and I told them 'no, I was sick.' I can't imagine what they were thinking. When I reached my bedroom, I felt eyes on me and I looked up and there was my mother standing behind me. I told her I was sick and at this point, I was. I was sick at my stomach and began to throw up a white foam in the floor. I made it to my bed and don't remember anything from that point. Later I was told the joint did indeed have PCP in it and I didn't have a clue what it was.

At 16, I had my own ride provided to me by my parents. This gave me the freedom to visit with all my partying friends. I would lie to my parents about where I was going and where I had been. I created my own secret life. I ran the streets buying pot and pills, using now on a daily basis. School was just a party as well. I would skip school with friends who used. We would ride around all day and get high. My grades went from decent to bad. I then got it in my head that I didn't have time for school and I wanted to quit. Instead, my Mom enrolled me in home school. I guess she knew I was hanging with the wrong kind of people and possibly that I was doing drugs. I made up lies about my friends to make them look good in my parents eyes so they wouldn't worry as much and maybe they'd think I was alright when I was gone.

Instead of graduating, I ended up getting my GED at 17 years old. Nothing seemed to matter to me at this point in my life. I had made myself a false reality. Thinking and feeling that I was fine and I was not addicted to anything. In reality, I was addicted to drugs, the crowd, the lies, the parties, and everything that was not good for me.

While I was 17, I was introduced to methamphetamine. I liked the high it gave me and there was plenty of it so I continued using it for a while. Having epilepsy and getting very little sleep wasn't good for my system at all. I began having grand-mal seizures more than normal. I remember the people I had been with being freaked out by my seizures. I became really afraid of what I didn't know. I asked one of the people at the house to take me to my doctor. When I got in to see him, I was honest with him about what I'd been doing. I was afraid not to tell him. I was young and not very smart about what risks I was taking. I recall my doctor's words to me. It was very startling for a 17 year old girl, and exactly what I needed to hear. He said simply, "Jennifer, if you continue to use crank, I will refuse to be your doctor, I will not be responsible for your death." I left his office feeling very shocked that what I had been doing could have this kind of consequence. Death, I was far from ready to meet my maker. I went home to my parents, slept it off and gained a little weight back, then hit the streets again. Living on a roller coaster ride seemed to be appealing to me. I went back to my 'old pot head buddies' and refused crank for awhile.

When I was 18, I met the guy I would end up marrying. He seemed really cool to me. Always talking about being in prison and selling drugs. Why this was appealing to me, I don't know. I guess it was the life I had surrounded myself with and maybe I felt like I had nothing better to do. I married him at age 19. We had a lot in common. We both enjoyed drugs and we were both liars. We lied to people to make ourselves sound good, or so we thought. We spent most of our time together partying.

He had a daughter who was about 4 or 5 years old. She was wonderful. She came to live with us in a house my parents provided for us. I wasn't a good mother. I didn't have a clue how to be a mother. I was still a girl myself. I recall the good times I spent with her. We would sing songs together and sometimes read books and watch movies. We played in the yard together. She was kind of like my life sized barbie doll. I also remember the bad times. People would come over to get high with us and we would send her outside to play by herself or with the kids they brought with them. I remember telling her "the things me and your daddy do in this house is no one's business, and if anyone ever asks you if me and your daddy smoke pot or do drugs, you tell them you don't know what they're talking about." She would ask me on occasion why we didn't want people to know we smoked pot. I simply told her some people don't do it and would have us put in jail. She already feared jail. She had seen her daddy taken away several times by the police already. This enforced that fear in her mind.

As the years went by, we began doing crank again. This time it was much different than ever before. Crank was becoming very abundant here in our small town. It was everywhere. My husband and a friend of his began taking trips to Atlanta bringing back large quantities. Plenty to sell, have your own stash and entertain all the visitors we had. Money was really never made. We couldn't stay out of the profit long enough to make any money. My mother had helped me acquire a local music store in the midst of all this, which I lost due to poor management. We did crank and sold it out of the store, right in the middle of town. Never even considering what would happen to us if we were caught.

During this time, my cousin whom I was very close to started staying with us a lot. His dad was an alcoholic and they would get drunk and fight a lot. I remember a time when he called me late one night and told me he was hiding in the parking lot of a local textile mill. He and his dad had gotten into a fight and he took off. I went and picked him up and kept him with me in the middle of a bunch of drug addicts. He began using as well. He was only 14 years old at the time.

My marriage went down hill. My husband began using the needle. We were both so strung out we didn't know which way was up or down. I filed for divorce. I thought I would still be able to see the daughter I had spent the last 5 years with because during these years I had adopted her. During the divorce hearing, I was told that his divorce from his previous wife was not finalized until after we were married. This left me with an invalid marriage and a voided adoption. I had no legal rights to her what-so-ever. I was devastated. I had lost her.

I remember the day they took her away. I cried for hours, holding her, telling her that no matter what, I would always love her. When she was gone, I went home where we had lived. I found my husband's bag of syringes. I sat at my kitchen table and began firing dope. A friend of mine came to see me. I was sitting there with a needle hanging out of my arm. My mind felt like it was on Mars. He asked me what had I done. I remember telling him, "they took her, she's gone, I have nothing more to live for." I went into a rage and busted up my house, breaking every- thing I could get my hands on. After everything was destroyed, I took it all outside and began to burn everything.

I continued to use the needle, spiraling downhill. Now that my husband was gone, I became the driver for the trips to Atlanta. This opened a big door to hell for me. I had cash given to me for the drive and plenty of dope. I think back now and realize if we had gotten stopped by the police and searched, the guys with me would've never claimed the dope. They would've either said it was mine or they didn't know who it belonged to, leaving me, as driver and owner of the car, to blame. My mind was so clouded by chemicals, the thought never even entered my mind.

I became a very violent person somewhere along this line. I was arrested for fighting a couple of times. My mother and brother signed papers to have me put in a hospital. They saw the needle tracks on my arms and the chemical look in my eyes. It didn't help. It only made me want more dope and become more violent. Doing more harm to myself than anyone.

I recall staying very depressed and very angry. All I thought about was getting more dope and when would I get my next fix. I began ripping people off for their money. Lying to people, telling them I'd get them dope if they gave me the money, and then never returning with dope or money.

I remember during all this mess, seeing my mother out on the road in the middle of the night, and thinking to myself 'what in the hell is she doing out at this time of night?' Well, a mother who loves her daughter very much was, of course, out searching for me. Spending sleepless nights looking for the daughter she feared would die.

I met Butch somewhere along the line. He became my lifeline to sanity. He knew just how bad I was and at first he didn't want me around. I refused to go when he told me to. He put me in my place a few times by reminding me that life didn't have to be the way I was living it. I would go to his house when I was down, needing rest and comfort. I would sleep for days at a time. He only woke me to give my medicine and make sure I ate. When I would wake up from the long sleep, I remember telling him I had to go to the store and would see him later. I would stay gone 2 or 3 weeks doing dope. Then I'd return again for rest. Somehow, he grew to love the girl underneath the monster I had become. My mom would call him sometimes to help her look for me. He was her only link to me.

While I was on one of my trips, I was given a drug, and to this day I don't know what it was, but I wound up sexually abused. I remember after I fired the shot, I felt drunk instead of geeked up. I blacked out in Armuchee and woke up the next day in Trion with no clothes on, beside a man I barely knew. He only told me, "I didn't do anything you didn't want me to do." I left and went to a friend's house and told them what happened. Their response was "well, you shouldn't have went up there to get him." I felt like a fool. This only added to my depression.

I went and found some cocaine because I couldn't find any crank at the time. I filled my needle with what I thought was enough to end all the misery. I remember every feeling just like it was yesterday. I fired the shot. My heart began pounding. My head was so hot I thought it would explode. My legs felt like jello. The girl in the car with me kept asking me, "are you allright, Jennifer?" It was like someone took a dimmer switch and slowly turned it off. I began praying in my mind. "God, please don't let me die, I only thought I wanted to die, God, please."

A while later, I'm not really sure how long, I came back to myself. I got up and started walking thru the parking lot of the pool hall I was at. I looked over at the entrance and saw my mother's truck pulling in. I knew in my mind I was probably wild eyed and needed to get her out of there. I walked over to her and I don't recall what I said but she left. Later she told me that I had told her I would come up to her office and talk to her. Of course, I never showed up. She also told me she had woke up in the middle of the night seeing only my face and that's why she came out looking for me. This was kind of a turning point for me. I knew I had to do something. I was dying inside. My physical health was awful. I only weighed about 100 pounds and my face was so skinny and sunk-in looking. I looked like walking death.

After another couple of months of wanting to quit but not being able, I remember feeling like a ton of bricks had been laid on my shoulders. The want and need to quit using was stronger than ever before. I started to Butch's house. I passed his house and his dad's truck was there. I didn't want him to see me in the shape I was in so I passed by and went down to the bridge on Hwy. 100 and sat there and cried. When I went back, I told Butch I had to quit. I'm sure he had a hard time believing me. I had told him the same thing before. Still, he didn't turn me away. I went in and went to sleep and slept for hours and hours, it seemed. He called my mom to tell her I was there and I was alright for the time being. I'm sure she was comforted by this call.

The struggle began. I wanted to use. I stayed frustrated and was feeling bad all the time. Butch would take me fishing, out to eat, riding old dirt roads in his truck, anything to get it off my mind. He tried so hard to help me. In the end, he did succeed. He was a blessing sent to me from God above. He became my very best friend and the man I love. He knew all the bad and the good. I didn't have to lie and keep things from him. He already knew.

Finally, I went home to my parents and Butch moved in with me. I started having 4 and 5 or more grand-mal seizures a month. I was sometimes unable to walk to the bathroom, and he would carry me. I started seeing my doctor again. He tried 3 or 4 different medicines for my seizures before we found one that would work. He said the damage I had done to my system could possibly be permanent. He was unsure at the time. My metabolism had changed so much that the medicines weren't working. This went on for 8 months. I recall nightmares I would have while getting clean. It seemed as though I dreamed of all the things I feared most. I dreamed my step-daughter died in my arms. I had dreams of sitting with using friends and firing shots. I would wake up scared to death thinking I had slipped up and gotten back on dope.

I recall wanting dope. I would have a bad day and begin thinking there was no point in staying off dope. When I felt this way, I would go out in the yard and I moved flowers from one part of the yard to another or brush my horse's hair for hours. Anything I could do to get it off my mind and make it thru the bad days.

I began counseling, which was a gateway for me to release some of the feelings I had to an ex-addict and very educated man (my counselor). I felt like he was a good counselor simply because he had been an addict himself. He'd had the same nightmares in the past. He dealt with the feelings of not wanting to carry on. He was able to give me the insight into myself that I needed to stay straight. He helped me a lot.

Finally the seizures stopped and I was beginning to lead a normal life that I hadn't known since I was just a little girl. I became closer to my family than ever before. I started spending time at my mother's office during the day. Beginning to have a new life was a whole new experience for me. I had no friends anymore other than my family, Butch, and Kelli. They were all I needed. All the old friends started calling me 'police' and things of this nature, which is normal. It never mattered to me. I knew I could make it as long as I didn't give in and go out and use. I had become a stronger person than I ever thought possible.

Since all the time has passed, I have helped a few peopple get clean which is a wonderful feeling for me. I never believed I'd be able to help anyone. My cousin that I spoke of earlier was one of those. He's clean today. He and I are close in a very different way than before. I am so proud of him. He's a wonderful young man today, and he is clean.

Even though I've been clean a year and a half, I have found there are still consequences and worries. Just a couple of months ago I received a letter from a friend I used with, telling me he was infected with hepatitis C which he contracted while sharing needles. I went for the test right away. The test itself wasn't scary, but the wait on the results just about drove me insane. I tried hard not to think about it. The morning I got off work and went to get the results, all I could think about was all the people I had shared needles with and all the people I had sex with during that time. The reality of all the danger I had put myself in was setting in hard once again.

For whatever reason, God saw fit for me to live a healthy life. He spared me one more time. All the tests were negative. The thought of this is very humbling for me. I could have easily died. I am nothing short of blessed.

Thru the years, I have seen 7 of my young friends laid to rest because of drug and alcohol related incidences. I am blessed to have this second chance at life. I have learned that I cannot take things for granted anymore. People in our lives and situations can disappear just as quickly as they were laid in front of us. None of us are promised anything, not even the next breath we take.

I have attended a lot of NA and the twelve steps have really helped me. I have also helped our local resource officer, Clint Young, on occasion, in presenting his meth lab presentation. It is wonderful education for the public. It tells you the true dangers of people cooking crank in homes, buildings and vehicles around you. It also lets you see the cost to the people of this county for cleaning up labs and the price changes in stores to make up for the loss when people go in and steal ingredients to cook meth. If you haven't seen the presentation, you should. The reality of it is scary but true. If the dangers of meth don't scare you, it certainly should. It is scary and dangerous and it is reality.

I went to a couple of presentations with Clint, to public places where I saw people who were on meth, and didn't seem to know why they were there. It's not hard for an addict to pick another one out of a crowd. Especially when you have a passion for being part of making a big change, like I do. My outlook has changed considerably over the past couple of years.

Today I feel like education is the key for our youth. Catch them while they're small and give them an understanding of the dangers of addiction. With drugs come addictions, then there's diseases, physical and sexual abuse, and even death. As far as helping the ones we love to get better, be there for them when they get down. Give them the moral support they need. Don't support their habits. Just let them know that when they're ready to quit, you'll be there. I'm sure it's very frustrating trying to love someone whose life is overcome with addiction. I feel that the parents, husbands, wives, and children of addicts have a much tougher time than the addict themselves. Someone you love is destroying themself and there seems to be no way for you to reach this person. It's got to be tough. Families are destroyed everyday because of drugs. Children are placed with foster families or other places while their parents go to prison or to their grave. I pray for them all. My mother had people that that don't even know me praying for me. No one can make me believe that there is no God and that He doesn't answer prayers. He answers prayers even if you don't attend church. God is a great and merciful God. He has shown me that. He had mercy on me and my family. If you don't believe that praying for your loved one will work, then it won't work. Have some faith. What else do you have ? Everything in our lives happens for a reason. Whether it's good things or bad things. They all have purposes. Drugs are here to stay, they're not going away. Every single person will not be able to be reached. One single victory in the fight against drugs is a wonderful feeling. I am a survivor and I am very proud of myself. All the lack of self confidence I had when I was using is gone. I am confident that I am a good person. I have realized that it doesn't matter what others think of me. When I meet my maker, I will be answering for myself and no one else. I am no longer afraid of dying. I have nothing to fear. God gave me a second chance and I'm going to let Him use me as His tool to help others. I pray there will be others who will survive this battle. To the families of addicts, God bless you.

Betty's Story

I am but one of many mothers who have struggled with the nightmare of seeing their child addicted to methamphetamines. I wouldn't wish this on anyone. It is, without a doubt, the worst experience of my life, and the most trying. My daughter, thank God, has survived and gone on to try to help others who are suffering. It is only thru the grace of God that she did survive. Many, many prayers were said on her behalf. He heard, and He saw fit to restore her to good health. Perhaps He had a bigger plan for her life. I thank Him every day for bringing my daughter back.

When Jennifer's problem first began, she hid it from me. Apparently, it had gone on for some time before I realized her problem. She was an adult, and even though I have always loved her more than my own life, I tried not to dominate her. I had made that mistake when she was a child. It wasn't because I wanted to run her life. Rather, it was because I wanted to protect her from the bad things in life. I, myself, had suffered greatly in my youth, and my maternal side compelled me to try to shield her. I realize now that too much unconditional love can have its pitfalls, just as lack of love or immature parenting can.

She had gone thru tremendous emotional pain, and when she "disappeared" I felt that she just wanted time alone. I tried to respect her privacy. However, bad things were happening with her. As with all meth addicts, she did not see it as a problem. It became her way of life. She went from a striking beauty to an almost skeletal creature that rarely slept or ate. Her "friends" and constant companions were people I could never understand her attraction to. Most of them were dirty looking, unkempt people who had no home, and seemed to live off of others. They struck me as "users" , though I didn't quite apply that term correctly at the time. I could not believe she preferred their company to the comfort of her own home.

I had been told by a few people that she was developing quite a bad drug problem. I was told that she was "shooting up" and I confronted her with it. She actually admitted it to me. She claimed the needle was the safest way to use the drug. She said she was addicted and didn't know if she could quit. She cried a few times and told me she wanted to quit. I knew in my heart she was telling the truth. But an even bigger truth was the fact that meth had her in it's grasp. She was highly dependent on the drug. I begged her to accept help through counseling, but she rejected. I begged her to come home. There were times when we cried together. A few times, she let me hug her while we both cried. I begged her to let me help her. Her heart said yes, but the addiction kept pulling her back.

Our close emotional bond had been there since she was born. However, she forgot about even that during this time. I didn't, and there were many nights when I would awaken and sit straight up, seeing her face right in front of me. I knew something was terribly wrong with her. I had no idea where she was. I would start praying as I climbed into my auto and began my midnight search. My prayer was always, "Father, please spare her life, please let her live, please bring her home." I would drive and look, though most of the time, I was blinded by tears. And, most of the time, my search was fruitless. She did not want to be found. I would drive and hunt for hours, and when I finally gave up the search, I would go on to work and try not to think. Always, in the back of my mind, was my constant prayer, "Father, please......."

One night I had rode and looked, and did actually spot her car, hidden behind a house I was not familiar with. At 2 a.m., I was trespassing on somebody's property. I drove as close as I could get to her car, then walked up and opened the passenger door. In my mind, again, was "Father, please......"

She was slumped behind the wheel and did not realize my presence. I sat down in the car and reached for her wrist to check for a pulse. I held my fingers under her nose to feel for warm breath. Thank God, she was alive. I sat there with her, and cried my heart out. I asked God why was this happening to her. I told God I loved her dearly, and I begged Him again to spare her. I told God I did not understand meth or how it had taken control over her. I prayed for knowledge and understanding. I wanted to be able to help her. I knew if I lost her, it would be the end of me as well. There would be no reason to go on.

This went on for some time, and I kept most of my pain inside, except when it spilled over out of my eyes. There were few people I could actually talk to about it. I knew others were suffering the same as we were, but it seemed nobody wanted to talk about it. The subject of meth was taboo. When I would hear of someone dying because of meth, I would cry for days. I knew someone's heart was broken. There was a void that would never be filled in their life. And why? Because of methamphetamines. Such a popular and deadly drug. Why were so many falling victim to it? What was the appeal? What was the answer?

The turning point came when she visited me at work one day. I had called one of her "buds" and told them if I didn't see her face or hear her voice by sundown, I would be filing a missing person's report and have a lookout posted on her car. She showed up a few hours later, angry and belligerent. She told me it was her life and I needed to leave her alone and forget about her. I looked deeply into her eyes, and I could see the chemicals. I also saw a demon, glaring at me, gloating and telling me "I've got her, and there's nothing you can do about it." Then and there, I realized the creature in front of me was not my daughter anymore. She left in a huff, but I had seen the situation for what it really was. Satan had my daughter. This was war, spiritual warfare, and Satan knew he could hurt me most by taking her from me. I thought, "if you want war, old boy, I'll give you war." I knew I finally had the knowledge I had prayed for. God had heard my prayers. He had opened my eyes to the truth. Now, I knew how to fight this fight. I sat down and made a list of people whom I knew were exceptionally strong in faith. At last, I knew how to fight it, but it would take strength to win this one. I actually had a game plan this time.

I made tearful phone calls to those good folks. Not that I wanted to cry to them, but the pain and fear boiled over. I asked them to please pray for Jennifer. They all said they would, and some said they would have their whole congregations pray for her. I felt the power of their prayers. I knew a force stronger than I was at work.

About a week later, she came home. She told me she was home to stay. She gave her keys to me and said, "This will be tough, but I'm through with it." She didn't leave the house for almost eight months, unless someone was with her. She told me she couldn't go out of the house. Home was her refuge, her safe haven. Nobody could reach her unless we wanted them to. She rested and slept a lot and her body and spirit began to heal. I remember one day when she was in bed, and I heard deep breathing coming from her room. I went to check on her, and heard a deep, horrible, moaning sound coming from inside her. I stood vigil, watching and praying. I knew in my heart the demons were leaving her body. They didn't go easy, but they went. When I heard their departure, I said "Go back to hell where you belong." I knew Jennifer had been delivered from evil. I had my daughter back. Through the Grace of God, she was delivered. I spent some time on my knees, thanking God. I knew He had broken the bonds. He had spared her life. There hasn't been a single day go by since then that I haven't said "thank you, Father."

Jennifer has been clean for more than 2 years now. She is healthy and happy. Her checkups show she was exceptionally fortunate to escape this plague with no lasting damage or disease. She was indeed one of the fortunate ones. Prayer saved my daughter. That's all there is to it.

Since her recovery and coming forth to talk about it, I have had numerous calls and visits from other parents, mostly mothers, going thru the same turmoil with their children. Sometimes, when I tell them it is spiritual warfare going on, they look at me like they think

I'm nutty. But they know, just as I do, that she is alive and well today thru the grace of God. I have found that, more than anything else, they need to talk. Sometimes, they need to cry. I tell them to let it out. I tell them prayer can move mountains and slay dragons.

Today, I am glad to share this testimony. I am glad to see the truth about meth being explored and exposed. Hiding the problem only advances the devil's cause. Expose him, stand up to him, and he will flee like the lying coward he is. His power can't hold a candle to the power we have thru Jesus Christ. We can win this fight, one precious person at a time. There is nothing more powerful in our entire universe than the living God. And together, we can move mountains.

Crystal Meth

I destroy homes, I tear families apart.
I take children and that's just a start.
I'm nore valued than diamonds, more precious than gold.
The sorrow I bring is a sight to behold.
If you need me, remember, I'm easily found.
I live all around you, in school and in town.
I live with the rich, I live with the poor.
I live just down the street, and maybe next door.
I'm made in a lab, but not one like you think.
I can be made under your kitchen sink,
Or in your child's closet, or even out in the woods.
If this scares you to death, it certainly should.
I have many names, but there's one you'll know best.
I'm sure you've heard of me. My name's Crystal Meth.
My power is awesome. Try me, you'll see.
But if you do, you may never break free.
Try me just once, and I might let you go.
Try me twice and I'll own your soul.
When I possess you, you'll steal and you'll lie.
You'll do what you have to do, just to get high.
The crimes you'll commit for my narcotic charms,
will be worth the pleasure you'll feel in my arms.
You'll lie to your Mother. You'll steal from your Dad.
When you see their tears, you mustn't feel sad.
Just forget your morals, and how you were raised.
I'll be your conscience. I'll teach you my ways.
I take kids from parents. I take parents from kids.
I turn people from God. I separate friends.
I'll take everything from you, even your good looks and pride.
I'll be with you always, right by your side.
You'll give up everything. Your family, your home.
Your money, your friends. You'll be all alone.

I'll take and take 'til you've no more to give.
When I finish with you, you'll be lucky to live.
If you try me, be warned. THIS IS NOT A GAME.
If I'm given the chance, I'll drive you insane.
I'll ravage your body. I'll control your mind.
I'll own you completely. Your soul will be mine.
The nightmares I'll give you when you're lying in bed,
and the voices you'll hear from inside your head.
The shakes, the sweats, and the visions you'll see.
I want you to know, these are your gifts from me.
By then it's too late, and you'll know in your heart
that you are now mine, and we shall not part.
You'll regret that you tried me. They always do.
But you came to me, not I to you.
You knew this would happen. How many times were you told ?
But you challenged my power. You chose to be bold.
You could've said 'no' and just walked away.
If you could live over, now what would you say ?
My power is awesome, as I told you before ....
I can take your Mother and turn her into a whore.
I'll be your master. You'll do as I say.
Even when I tell you to go to your grave.
Now that you've met me, what will you do ?
Will you try me or not ? It's all up to you.
I can show you more misery than words can tell.
Come, take my hand .... Let me lead you to hell.

    Anonymous

CHAPTER ONE

Early Years

From the day she was born, Jennifer was a bundle of joy. She was precious and beautiful, and loved beyond measure by me, her dad and big brother Jim. She was my baby doll, and I loved dressing her in velvet and lace. Everyone would gush over my rosey cheeked baby girl when I took her to church or on outings. Her smile stole the show.

Unfortunately, the umbrella of real love that she enjoyed was basically her immediate family. Beyond that, dysfunctional is about the only way to describe our extended families. Since I can't say much that's good here, I will say nothing at all. Lessons in wisdom have taught me this.

Actually, my dad doted on her, but he was seldom around. She loved him, too. He was " Paw Paw " the undisputed one and only. Jennifer treasured the time she could spend with him. She had a great grandmother that loved her dearly, too, but age and health problems limited her tremendously. Beyond that, it was just us.

For all practical purposes, however, she was our priceless little princess and the apple of her big brother's eye. She thought he hung the moon, and he loved the 'big brother' role. She was the deeply loved daughter and sister, and it could be that we spoiled her somewhat.

Hindsight tells me I might've tried too hard to compensate for other shortages in her life. I know that I tried. Then again, maybe I'm trying to rationalize why she turned to drugs at all. I struggle with the theory that it's usually peer pressure. Perhaps it truly is, but a mother always wonders what went wrong. The eternal question for many Moms seems to be 'why did this happen to my child?' How many times have I heard that from a devastated parent? For that matter, how many times have I cried out the same words, followed closely by fervent pleading that Jennifer's life be spared. I lost count many tears ago.

There is one thing I will never stop believing, and that is that God heard my prayers and all the prayers being said for her. He spared Jennifer's life and made her better than before. Could it be that He wanted us to appreciate this blessing enough to reach out to other hurting souls? It's very possible.

He would've known the evil that was spreading across our land, and what a tremendous need there would be for hope and comfort. Truly, I have never felt so helpless in my entire life as when I tried to fight this faceless demonic substance that threatened her life. Just the fact that I opposed it, and tried to hinder her from getting it, caused her to see me as the enemy. Meanwhile, the ones who were supplying her were the ones she adored. No, I have never fought an enemy like this one before, and I hope I never do again. It brought me to my knees. Both of us were lucky to survive this ordeal.

Meth is a faceless coward, creeping up on unsuspecting souls, delivering power punches that the user doesn't anticipate, and is in no way prepared to handle. This is just one of many visions of knowledge that came to me on this journey to recovery.

Jennifer has told me that her very first experience with any type drug came when she saw her brother and his friends slipping into a wooded area to share a 'joint.' Her dad had always told her, 'that stuff will kill you, don't fool with it.' My input was simply, 'don't do it.' When she realized what her brother was doing, she paniced and started screaming at him. "No, Jim, don't do it, you'll die."

When the boys convinced her no one was going to die and this was just a scare tactic from good-ole-dad, her feelings changed about the 'forbidden' stuff. After all, if her brother was doing it, it must not be too bad. She reasoned that she would try it, too, sooner or later. She had no way of knowing, at that time, that she would be opening a door and it would lead to almost fatal consequences for her. Actually, seven of her young friends did pay with their life thru drug related incidents or accidents. After her recovery, and when the fog was gone from her mind, she would grieve her heart out for those young lives that were lost. I've heard her sob, "they didn't get another chance."

At times, she even struggled with guilt feelings. Guilt because she was alive and they weren't. She had a hard time coming to terms with the fact that she was spared and given another chance, while others weren't. She failed to find the wisdom or fairness in this. I thought about it, too, and I knew that, but for the grace of God, we would be the same. Everyday, I always made a point to say 'thank you' for her life. I knew we couldn't do anything about her lost friends, other than try to make a difference for younger ones bringing up their footsteps.

CHAPTER TWO

On We Go

As she grew older, new problems surfaced and changes needed to be made. A different school in a neighboring county, with new friends, seemed to be called for. This was a good idea. However, it was not without problems, and within a few short months, I felt the need to withdraw her. We opted for home school. At the time, I was on medical leave from my job, so I had time to devote to her education. It was approved through our local board of education, and so we began home schooling.

She was in a new world, so to speak. Phone calls were not allowed. Neither were visits during school hours. She never left my sight. Later, she would tell me that most of what she studied went right over her head. Still, within just a few months, she was ready to take her GED test. She passed, actually doing very well on her first try. She felt educated.

During this time, she was enrolled in modeling classes, too. I thought this would be good for her self esteem, and she seemed to enjoy it immensely. She took trips to places like Los Angeles, the Carolinas, and Atlanta for modeling conventions and photo shoots. She won 'call backs' and several photogenic awards. She won several beauty pageants, too.

My hope was that these experiences would strengthen her self confidence. They were expensive investments, but all were intended to try to help her. Try as we might, the drug culture existed even in these areas. It seemed that every way she turned, there were new suggestions being sent her way, and many of them involved drugs, alcohol, or illicit sexual acts. She was being pulled toward the drug culture, and there was little I could do to fight it. She was by no means the only one. It was like some evil magnet was luring our youth, and it came from several different angles.

When she was close to eighteen, Jennifer met a young man whom she really seemed to 'take to.' She felt sure she'd met her life mate. I don't doubt that she loved him very much. We all know how fragile and susceptible the young female heart can be, and she was hungry for a stable relationship. Truthfully, she was still very immature, perhaps even maladjusted. I knew this was inevitable. It was an affair of the heart, and I could not protect her from herself this time. She saw him through the eyes of young love.

I saw him as a young man with very little education, and even less initiative to work and try to build a home. I suspect he had never known much of a home life. He told us he had spent time briefly in prison. He also had a three year old daughter that his collective family was raising. The birth mother had given up the child and went her way, he said.

The young child was brought to visit several times, and after he and Jennifer married, she came to live with them. She was very precious, with long curly locks, big brown eyes, and such a sweet personality. She was hungry for parental love. This showed in all her actions. She started calling Jennifer 'Mama' right away, and this pleased Jennifer very much. Interestingly enough, she never met a stranger, although she was quite frightened by police. The only explanation I heard was that she'd seen her daddy handcuffed and taken away several times. Police were always made out to be the 'bad guys.' She would tremble when she heard police sirens and I've seen her run and hide from uniformed officers. It was amazing to see a three year old little girl do this.

However, it wasn't hard to remedy that problem. Here in Summerville we have some very 'kid friendly' cops and I introduced her to some of them. She quickly changed her mind and at times she would run to them and wrap around their legs when she saw them in public. Our super nice police chief gave her an official cap for her sixth birthday along with a tour of the department. She loved him but didn't care for the loud truck horns. She told me several times that she'd like to be a police officer when she grows up.

The three of them lived in various residences for awhile, and finally would up living close to us. I've heard she and Jennifer singing songs together and playing on a swing set. Jennifer would read stories to her and they both enjoyed it immensely.

I wish I could say all was well and good from that point on, but it wasn't. Still, there is nothing to be gained in throwing mud or rehashing painful times, so we won't go there. Let's just say things did not work out for the best, and after five very unstable years, it was over and Jennifer had to give up the child.

This was truly the gut kick that sent her spiraling downward. The day the child left was intensely heartbreaking. It was so hard to see her cry and plead not to have to go. No one wanted her to leave, by any means, but we had no choice. A judge made the decision that blood was the deciding factor. So, the father was awarded custody, and since he was in detention at the time, his daughter would be sent, at least temporarily, to live with the birth mother. The last words I could say to the child, other than telling her we love her very much, was simply 'don't forget Summerville.' Her reply was " I won't, and I love all of ya'll, too.' I believe the time will come when she will find her way back, and she will be welcomed with open arms. Every single day, I ask God to take care of her and keep her safe. This was heart wretching, hurting to the bone.

Jennifer was beyond consolation over her loss. She fell deeper and deeper into depression. She felt she had lost everything and the secrecy veil lifted. She simply didn't care anymore, and she turned to methamphetamine for her mood enhancer. I started finding out things I hadn't known before, such as, she was adept at firing up a needle. About a year or so later, she confessed in front of about

150 people, including me, that she knew how to cook meth, too. Evidently, marriage had been quite a learning experience for her, and she was well educated in the drug art. The fact that she just didn't care anymore amounted to double trouble.

For all practical purposes, she disappeared into the drug world. She would come home on occasion, but most of the time I had no idea where she was or whom she was with. I did recognize that she was an adult, albeit a very traumatized young one. Legally, she could make her own decisions. It was generally a waste of time and effort trying to keep up with her. I learned there are countless hiding places available to people who don't want to be found.

This was a time of intense worry for me, but I tried to back off and let her have her space. In a sense, I felt like she needed this, but I was not comfortable, considering some that I knew she was hanging out with. It was cause for great concern.

This is truly one of the toughest times for any parent. Love and concern says you need to do your best to help them through this. When they are adults, and demanding to be left alone, what do you do? Is there an even ground where you can let them know you're there for them, but not dominating them? What about the terrible addiction they're getting deeper into? Common sense tells us it's only going to get worse. There's always the dangers of overdose, bad dope, having something slipped to them, and all the other nightmarish things we hear about. That doesn't include problems they'll face if they get caught with the stuff, or dangers from accidents that happen frequently with drug induced minds. A concerned parent's mind can cover most all worries, while our offspring's fogged mind doesn't seem to comprehend at all.

I know many parents who've made the painful decision to back out of the way. For many, their very sanity required it. It was just too mentally and physically exhausting to deal with it on a day to day basis. Was the decision to 'cut the cord' so to speak, the right thing to do? I'm certainly not the judge.

I will say, without hesitation, that when I didn't know her whereabouts and was sick with worry, I learned to pray fervently. Believe me, I learned the power of prayer.

I want to emphasize that before this happened, I was not that big on prayer. Sure, I had been to church, numerous times. I'd heard countless sermons. I had prayed, and been baptized. I'd taken my children with me, but it was very taxing to get up on Sunday morning and do all that had to be done, plus get them ready, and go. Discouraging might be a better description. I remember thinking there should be a law requiring daddy's to take their children to church. It would be good if there was, but we all know it's not going to happen. Unfortunately, it often falls on the mother to do this by herself. And was it my imagination, or are mothers with small children, and minus the daddy, treated differently, perhaps inferior or even cold, in some churches?

Sometimes, it's easier to just give up the fight than to fight it all by yourself. That's just about what I'd done, so I could understand her dilemna.

Still, I was helpless in this fight. I couldn't make her listen or do anything, for that matter. When I tried, we usually ended up yelling at each other. I understand how it feels to want to hug your child with one hand, to tell them you love them and would do anything to help them. At the same time, the other hand wants to slap their face for causing us so much agony. And why is it that we are the ones trying the hardest to help them, and they see us as the enemy? So many of them think they don't have a problem at all, except the ones they accuse us of creating for them.

When they're on dope, they never tire of mean, ugly, and vile things to say to us and about us. They tell people we're terrible. They curse us to our backs and sometimes to our face.

They will take from us, take advantage of us, destroy us monetarily, wreck our health, break our hearts, and blame us for all of it. Still, a parent who truly loves will not give up on their child. It might be that all we can do is pray fervently and ask others to do the same. Don't ever think that prayer doesn't work. Don't think you are not being heard. If you do it humbly, and with due reverence, you will be heard.

Then you must trust God to take it from there. 'Let go and let God' as most of us have heard. He sees more than we do. He knows more than we, and He can do anything. The Bible says, 'all things are possible with God.' We mustn't get impatient if things don't happen like we think they should, or as quickly as we'd like. I've learned thru this awful experience to trust Him and keep praying, plus do all I can to keep myself in check, and He will do the rest, and even more than I've asked for.

Before all this, I didn't know what a close relationship with God was, or how it felt. I do now, and I never want to lose it or give it up. He promised He would never leave me, and He keeps His promises. I don't deserve anything this wonderful, this truly good. In fact, I don't deserve much of anything. I certainly didn't earn it. Grace is what it's called, and it's a free gift. As I draw closer, my purpose becomes clearer. I know what He wants me to do. And do it, I will. I have no fear. Mighty angels have been sent to protect me from harm and evil. I will trust my God to make all things well. Is this what 'faith so simple a child can understand means ?'

Chapter Three

Love and War

After the worst of Jennifer's recovery was past, and we became known for our efforts against meth, we had many visitors. Notably, most of them were young women who were wanting to break free of the drug, and of course, there were many parents, mostly mothers. From talking with these young women, it became apparent that most of them were introduced to it by their boyfriend or husband. We came to understand it was a tool used to keep the female under their control. Once the female was addicted, she would do absolutely anything to get her 'fix.' Some suppliers would brag and laugh about the things they would coerce the girls into doing. It was sad and at the same time, sickening. Still, these girls would follow any orders, perform any sex act, steal or fight as they were instructed, basically do whatever it took to get the drug they were convinced they had to have.

They would cling to their suppliers, and / or 'cookers', and would lose most or all of their concern for anything or everything else, including children and parents. Sadly, most of the time these young women were so blinded by the chemical buzz that they did not even realize they had a serious problem. Experience showed that in most cases, it would take a big wake-up call to get their attention and make them see what they were doing to themselves. Most terrible of all is when we lost them permanently.

I must admit I have wept buckets of tears over several of Jennifer's friends, many of whom I never met. Whether I knew them personally was of little consequence. The fact is, they had a mother that loved them dearly. At least, I hope they did. Only a mother's heart can hold so much love, and feel such depths of pain and grief. My heart bleeds for all who've lost their child.

I recall one particular death that left me weeping for days. I was listening to the police scanner one day when I heard the call go out for assistance to a mother who was performing CPR on her grown daughter. The mother had found her in what was apparently a near death state. She frantically called for help. The EMT's and police arrived and took over her efforts. Nothing worked. The mother was present when an EMT came over the radio saying, 'there's nothing we can do here.' My blood just chilled over those words.

It was horrible news, and I felt hot tears stinging my eyes and face. I did not know the identity of the girl at that time, but the very thought of the mom having to go thru this was heart- wretching. Later, I found that the dead girl was indeed a friend of my daughter's. Not only that, she was young and very pretty and hooked on drugs. What a waste of human life. My tears burned for days over this one.

As drug abuse reports increased in our community, so did my fear and concern over Jennifer's safety. I started keeping up with local statistics and news much more than before. In our town, the actual cause of death was rarely given thru local news outlets. It was thru word of mouth the community was able to keep up with local drug deaths.

Just a few heartbreaking examples include one man both Jennifer and I knew. He was in his early fifties, and well known for his friendly manner. He had abused alcohol for many years, then added meth, intravenously, to his misery. He reportedly used dirty needles and contracted a staph infection. It got to the point that machines were required to do certain bodily functions for him. Tiring of this, he made the conscious choice to turn off his machine.

We heard of another victim who contracted aids from needles and died as a result. This was publicly called a 'blood disorder' and of course, it was. Chemically caused, however.

Another very disturbing death was of a very handsome young man who, like most others, had fallen victim to meth. He was a cooker, and had conjured up a batch. Reportedly, all his cohorts were waiting for the 'goods' but this time it didn't look right. The cook knew it, and from all accounts, he decided to be the tester. This was a big mistake, and sadly, it was his last one. He fell into a coma and remained for months. He succumbed.

Another case was of a beautiful young sixteen year old girl, much like my daughter had been. Wanting to fit in with certain crowds, she went along with the drug culture. She came from a fine family who loved her dearly, but they were powerless to stop her abuse. There was a boyfriend involved, and I found out later, he was an ex boyfriend of my daughter's. Her brief and precious life ended at sixteen. I never met this young girl, and did not know her family personally, but that didn't hold back my tears. They flowed for days. This was so terrible, so permanent.

At least three of Jennifer's friends died from auto accidents which were attributed to drugs and / or alcohol. One of the young girls had previously been a frequent overnight visitor in my home. I knew her well. She was a very sweet, loving girl with long and beautiful raven hair. I was told she was not driving. Both girls died almost immediately upon impact.

Another young man reportedly died when, as we heard it, his heart exploded from a lethal dose of meth. To this day, I don't believe his mother has recovered enough to get off medication. The last time I saw her, she needed help just maneuvering around Wal Mart.

One other young man died when he was thrown from his auto and it rolled over his body. I was told this was during a high speed chase by police. He was too impaired to handle his speed and lost control, and his life, in the process.

There were several others, but the stories are very similar. Such a loss, and such a waste. When I think of these lives that Satan has destroyed, and all the broken hearts that grieve over their loss, I can't help but weep. I usually just hide my face so no one will see my tears. They roll, and they burn, for the many victims of narcotics. One has to think, if it weren't for these heinous drugs and all that goes along with them, these people would probably be alive today. Many hearts would be jubulant instead of sad or medicated. I have to thank God everyday for sparing my daughter's life.

I also thank him for allowing us to experience the joy of recovery which we see frequently. I recall one young mother of four children calling me from work. She had been given my number by a co-worker. I didn't know the girl, but the pain in her voice was unmistakably clear. She said her skin felt like it was crawling. She had been off meth thirty days and was diligently trying to stay off it. She wanted to be a good mother to her children, but she was craving meth so badly. She felt like she was almost to the point of leaving her job and finding a 'fix.' Instead, she called me and we talked awhile. I could hear her crying and could almost feel the frenzy she was in. She gave me directions to her home and said she needed to talk more. Later that day, after she'd gotten home from work, I drove to her home to talk with her. I brought her a book which I've found to be most helpful to users and their families, called "Meth = Sorcery" by Steve Box. We talked awhile and I called my minister from my cell phone and had him talk with her, too. They prayed together. There was a "Conquerors for Christ' meeting that very night and she went to it. I knew she was really trying to clean up her act. Meth just didn't want to let go of her.

About a month later, this same young mother visited me. She looked great, with clear skin, shining eyes, and dressed with pride. She told me she was doing much better. She was about to start back to school. She talked about how happy her children and husband were to have her home, and how glad she was to be there. She is the young Mom I mentioned earlier, with reference to her youngest child calling her on a phone at her 'drug' house. He had tearfully told her, 'it doesn't matter if we have nothing to eat, Mama, just please come home.' He just wanted his Mom. Thank God, she came home to her family. Love won this round.

Yet another case that was close to home involved a young mother, again with four children involved. She'd married a man who was caught in the lure of dope and it's monetary benefits. She thought he was a real prize, and she was so proud for folks to know he was her man. The police found an active lab in their home. Her man could've spared her much agony, but he didn't. This brain washed young mother chose prison over co-operating with authorities. Of course, the children suffered more than anyone. They were hurt, confused, and displaced. Relatives, friends, and the state of Georgia picked up where she left off. Unfortunately, at least one of the children suffered such emotional trauma that she wound up in a special home / facility. This was the only place that could truly deal with her, and hopefully, help her to handle this situation. The children had no control, no voice, and they had to learn to go on without Mom. To this day, I don't believe she knows just how badly she hurt her children.

Through most of these occurences, and many more strikingly similar, meth was the underlying cause, the culprit, that brought such pain and agony to so many. For me personally, the worst part was seeing the innocent suffer. They didn't ask for this. For that matter, neither did the ignorant user who had no idea what just one 'hit' of meth could do to change their lives forever.

Would they really have started this vicious cycle if they'd known the grief that lay ahead ? Is any amount of chemical joy or camaradie with 'pals' worth this ? I think not.

We hear that education and public awareness is the real key to cracking meth, and I believe it. Further, I believe we need to alert and prepare our children before the dealers get to them. Our kids need and deserve advance preparation, which comes with a pro-active agenda. Telling them to 'just say no' is good, but I think we need to take it further.

Section Two

The Community Fights Back

A few months into recovery, Jennifer was inspired to try to help other users. She worried about them. Telling me that she understood their pain, and the hardship of addiction, she became somewhat driven to try to make a difference.

She was being shunned by all of her old 'user' friends. Her pet name with them was "Jennifer Police." They avoided her like the plague. She liked this, because, in a sense, it was easier for her to avoid temptation when it wasn't ' in her face. ' Slowly, and only after she overcame the physical hardships brought on by her changed metabolism, she was improving. She began making new friends, meeting new people, and basically expanding her horizons and improving her circle. I was witnessing new and pleasant personal growth patterns in my daughter. I was impressed.

Part of her metamorphisis was to work with members of our local police department, educating youth and the general public. Our city's police resource officer, Clint Young, quickly recognized the appeal she fostered. She accompanied him during school presentations, fire department and city hall meetings, plus citizen and church gatherings. Given the widespread concern of our 'clean' society members, these educational efforts were very well received.

Jennifer enjoyed these events immensely, and after much delay, I was able to sit in on a few. I had deliberately stayed away at first, being concerned that my presence might make her uncomfortable. It was very moving, to say the least. My daughter touched a lot of nerves. She told me privately that she could tell by watching faces and behavior, exactly who was and wasn't using the 'stuff.' She explained it to me, but I'm afraid I was far behind in the recognition game.

Another thing she felt led to do was begin a "Narcotics Anonymous" branch. She put a lot of time, effort, patience and understanding in this effort. I know that she helped several people. Even she benefitted from the 'twelve steps to recovery' program. She was undergoing other counseling at the same time. This was correctional counseling, and had been ordered by the court. She said this was tremendously helpful in getting her thru mood swings, cravings, unnerving dreams and other sensitive 'psyche' aspects. When she wasn't absorbing herself in these things, she was busy brushing her horse's hair, or transplanting flowers all over the yard. She was starting to enjoy life again, with a clean, clear head. This was so much improvement. I don't think I've ever seen my daughter so dedicated to anything worthwhile. It was almost like witnessing a rebirth. I was amazed and impressed.

As her progress continued, she and I crossed paths with numerous new people, from 'helpers' to 'hurters.' We heard so many stories, from all aspects of the meth menagerie. New and lasting friendships were begun.

Another effort we began was that of putting out informational brochures and anti-meth pamplets at various businesses and governmental locations. We began this as an experiment, because we weren't really sure how people would respond to having this information right under their noses. We found the data packs were picked up almost as quickly as we could keep them refilled. This was so encouraging. Various volunteers came forward, all wanting to help get this data out in their own communities. This was so encouraging. It told us that people were hungry for helpful know- ledge. People actually did want help. Our wheels were picking up steam. This was extremely motivating. We knew we were helping and it was going to make a difference.

Jennifer's first 'media' effort came when she wrote a heart- felt 'letter to the editor.' It became an open letter to the whole county. She was very frank about everything and our local editor, Gene Espy, presented it in a most effective manner. He also interviewed me for the parental aspect of her story, because she had given me so much credit for helping her thru this. She called it the 'constant vigilance' of her Mom that pulled her through. The story was very moving. I received several calls, visits and letters about the article. Several mothers called and cried over the phone. I want to add that Jennifer had mentioned that she felt the need to do this on at least three occasions before I offered any encouragement. After the third mention from her, I knew she felt a strong need. That's when I told her to call Gene Espy.

I'll also add that I dreaded the article. In fact, it was several days before I could bring myself to open the paper. I knew it was there from all the feedback I was getting. I simply could not force myself to look at it. Living thru the ordeal had been devastatingly taxing, and just the thoughts of reading about it was almost overwhelming. This was hard. I will say that Gene did a very good job. I could tell that his heart was in it. He felt our pain.

Following on the heels of this much-read letter and article, several others followed. They were so intriguing. Bittersweet might be the word to describe the feelings. There was so much pain involved, yet there was hope. The lights were coming on. Discussing the problem openly was good. Meth was now out in the open. Still 'taboo' terrible, but out there where we could beat up on it.

We will attempt to show some of our county and community's progress in the fight. The following articles testify to the passion we all felt. So many new alliances were formed, all with common ground to fight over. Our children are simply not expendable, and we won't give up without a battle. We will fight. I know that I have made so many new friends, and I respect them tremendously. Their dedication and tenacity make them stand out. Maybe they're just everyday heroes, or maybe they're exceptional citizen's. Either way, I'm glad I got to know the people who rose to the fight against meth.

The Summerville News

NUMBER XI. SUMMERVILLE, CHATTOOGA COUNTY, GEORGIA — THURSDAY, OCTOBER 17, 2002

STILL ONLY 25¢

A Mother's And Family's Love Helps Change A Life

Young Woman Decides To Try To Help Others That Are In Her Prior Predicament

Open Letter To Chattooga County Teens And Parents

Methamphetamine Study Committee
July 30, 2004   10:00 A.M.
Chattooga County Civic Center

Introduction to Meth:
>   Clint Young - Summerville Police Deptartment
>   Pat Cook - Lookout Mountain Drug Task Force

Welcome .Chattooga County Commissioner - Jim Parker

Introduction of Committee Members . . . . Rep. Barbara Massey Reece
>   Rep. Mike Snow
>   Rep. Curtis Jenkins
>   Rep. Howard Mosby
>   Rep. David Graves
>   Gardner Sapp, Research Analyst

Sgt. David Reeps . . . . Rome / Floyd Metro Drug Task Force
Charles "Dino" Richardson . . . . Lookout Mountain Drug Task Force
Ron Womack . . . . .City of LaFayette - Legal Counsel
Betty & Jennifer Brady . . . . .Community Volunteers
Brenda Taylor . . . . .Director, Dade County DFACS
Cathy Bitterman . . . . .State DFACS Liasion to GBI
Jesse Hambrick . . . . .Douglas County Drug Task Force

Hosted by . . . . The Chattooga County Chamber of Commerce
Sponsors . . . . BiLo - Scott Phillips, Manager
>   Carl Black Ford, Donnie Hall
>   Coca Cola, Robert Hitchcock
>   Georgia Power, Danny Fricks

6-A The Summerville News
Thursday, July 8, 2004

Law Officers: Meth Is Plaguing County

By D. J. LAAN
Staff Writer

Detective Pat Cook Addresses Meeting

Det. Pat Cook, Lookout Mountain Drug Task Force, at lecture, addresses a House of Representatives Study Committee on Meth in Summerville on June 30. Cook said Chattooga County is a hotbed of meth labs. (Staff Photo by D. J. Laan)

Meth Committee Hears Issues On Deadly Drug

More Than 150 Present For Study Session

By D. J. LAAN
Staff Writer

Rep. Barbara Reece, D-Menlo, chaired a Georgia House of Representatives committee in Summerville June 30th to discuss issues surrounding meth-amphetamine production, use and sale in Georgia. Four more hearings are scheduled in other parts of the state.

Rep. Howard Mosby, District 59, Post 5; Rep. Mike Snow, D-Chickamauga, and Gardner Sapp, a research assistant were on hand to listen to a large audience of more than 150 law enforcement officers, social workers, government officials and the public discuss issues about methamphetamine.

The meeting abruptly began as a casket was rolled into the main meeting room at the Chattooga County Civic Center. When the top cover was opened by Henry Mason, owner of Mason's Funeral Home, Summerville, containing meth lab ingredients in the front portion of the casket, some of the audience voiced surprise.

"That surely got a lot of attention," County Commissioner Jim Parker commented.

Public Resource Officer Clint Young, Summerville Police Department, then began to talk about the hazards of meth by using a power point presentation on a large screen television.

REP. REECE

Rep. Reece said the production and use of methamphetamine is a major problem in Northwest Georgia as well as one that is being felt in other parts of the state as well.

"I talked to families who have loved ones who are now addicts to meth. It is a disruptive, seductive drug that seems to sneak up on the user," she said, "who doesn't realize that he (she) is suddenly an addict."

Reece added that the average meth user isn't necessarily a stereotypical criminal but one who is often willing to divert to burglary or robbery as a result of using the drug.

"The public needs to know more about this drug. We need newspapers, the broadcast media, everyone with influence," she said, "to begin telling citizens about what they are up against."

Rep. Snow encouraged the media to tell as much as it possibly can about the problems with meth, also.

Reece added that there seems to be an ease in how easily meth 'cookers' are able to purchase ingredients.

"I hope to hear ideas from speakers and the public on how to control this problem," Rep.
see METH COMMITTEE, page 8-A

Community Leaders Discuss Meth Issues

More than 150 community leaders, law enforcement and the public met in Summerville June 30 to discuss methamphetamine's effects on Northwest Georgia. Standing behind a casket filled with meth ingredients is Chattooga County Sheriff Ralph Kellett, left, Rep. Mike Snow, Chickamauga, Rep. Howard A. Mosby, Atlanta, Rep. Barbara Reece, Menlo, Commissioner Jim Parker, John 'G. R.' Bankhead, GBI and Officer Clint Young, Summerville Police Department. The casket is furnished by Mason Funeral Home, Summerville. (Staff Photo by D. J. Laan).

Issues On Deadly Drug

More Than 150 Present For Study Session

from front page

Reece said.

She told The Summerville News that the ingredients needed to produce meth are currently legal to purchase in many retail stores.

SPEAKERS

Several speakers addressed the panel of legislators including Det. Pat Cook, Lookout Mountain Drug Task Force, Summerville Police Department Public Resource Officer Clint Young, Brenda Taylor, Director of Chattooga and Dade County's Department of Family and Childrens Services, Cathy Bitterman, Georgia DFCS liaison to the GBI, Jessee Hambrick, Douglas County Drug Task Force, Phil Price, District GBI director, Raymond Grossman, Whitfield County Narcotics Division, Vanita Hullander, Catoosa County coroner as well as Becky Jackson, E-911 and Lisa Hall, Trion Fire Department and Com. Jim Parker, Chattooga County.

Rep. Reece said several dignitaries attended the session but did not address the audience including Harris Childers, Georgia Div. of Paroles, Warden Steve Upton, Hays State Prison, John Heavener, Georgia Retail Association, Mike Hill, Harrabson/Paulding Drug Task Force, Kathy Floyd, Floyd County DFCS, Joe Adams, Georgia Dept. of Health, Betsy Quinn, Hutcheson Medical Center, and Ben Scott, Drug Enforcement Agency (DEA) in Charge of Chattanooga Region and Agent Frank Ledford.

Ann Davis, Highland Rivers Community Services, Floyd County attended.

Members of the public addressing the forum included Betty Brady, Jennifer Brady, Linda Pillow and Jimmie Pendergrass.

Local Law Enforcement represented included Chief Stan Mosley, Summerville Police Department, Sheriff Ralph Kellett and Chief Charles Latta, Trion. Several local police officers also attended the forum.

JENNIFER BRADY

Jennifer Brady, Summerville, whose story about meth was published last week in The Summerville News, told the panel, in response to a question from Rep. Snow about whether she believes her school, could have done more to help students fight drug addiction — that the answer is definitely "Yes."

"We weren't exposed to facts about drugs as we should have been. Facts about meth need to come from users not from education textbooks," she said.

She told legislators that there are too many prescription drugs with meth bases being administered to students in public schools in the county.

As she told her story about her own meth addiction, several members of the audience as well as the committee asked questions about her life story. "Why did this happen. How did it happen to you?" Rep. Snow asked her. "I wish I could tell you why. I honestly don't know," she replied. She added that she came from a middle class home with parents who loved her. She added that she was a good student but had low self-esteem and was shy.

When asked about how she finally defeated meth, Ms. Brady said she can only thank God and the constant vigilant help of her mother, Betty Brady, for her deliverance.

BRENDA TAYLOR

Brenda Taylor, director of Chattooga and Dade County Department of Family and Childrens Services, told legislators that her social workers are at risk because of meth contamination.

"This is such a new area that there have been no guidelines set to help us know what to do. The guidelines are being set daily, it seems," she said.

She noted that DFCS social workers are being called to the scene of manufacturing meth labs to take custody of minors found on the premises.

"Besides the issue of safety at the site of the lab, there is also a safety issue for a social worker making a friendly visit to a site," Taylor said "and suddenly coming in touch with a meth lab and toxic contamination."

She added that there are new concerns about contamination of vehicles and drivers of those vehicles used to transport children who have been taken from the immediate vicinity of a meth lab.

"We have decided that if we remove the clothing from the child immediately," she explained, "that it cuts the contamination exposure of residue to the worker down by as much as 80 to 90 percent."

DFCS is also dealing with proper methods to decontaminate transportation vehicles of children from meth lab areas.

Additionally, social workers are now taking children exposed to meth immediately to Children's Hospital in Chattanooga for emergency care, examination and evaluation.

"There's so many things that needs to be checked on these children. Blood data needs to be checked as well as bone density. Meth contamination affects these areas of the body," she explained.

Also, tests on the bones and teeth of children from meth environments must be monitored up to 12 months as the deterioration of their bodies can continue due to meth contamination.

"We have other issues such as how to help and educate foster parents who are caring for these children," she added.

SAFE HOMES

With the increasing number of safe homes needed for 'meth' children who have been removed by DFCS from methamphetamine lab locations, finding more people willing to offer foster care to the children is a must.

"We have problems now finding foster parents for other types of child cases. The meth epidemic here offers a new problem for us to house these children who are victims of meth abuse," Ms. Taylor added.

She added that the goal of DFCS has always been to eventually return children to their parents once a situation is alleviated.

"With the very risky statistics out today of whether folks can get off meth once they've been smokers," she said, "DFCS officials are faced with a dilemma about whether a child can ever be returned to these parents."

Ms. Taylor added that the cost to the taxpayer looms increasingly high as costs for continuing meth drug screens and other care factors are assessed by DFCS.

She noted that in 2003, 102 children were removed from Chattooga County homes due to drug manufacture or use/abuse of a parent.

"They are choosing meth over their children," she said.

Taylor noted that $48,000 was paid out in 2003 in Chattooga County to relatives who were caring for children who had been removed from their homes due to substance abuse cases.

"Ninety-percent of these cases are meth-related," she concluded.

Rep. Snow asked Taylor if she knew of any parents who have been given custody of their children, which had been removed because of meth abuse.

She responded, "No."

Some members of the audience showed that parental rights of meth parents should be revoked permanently.

SHERIFF KELLETT

Rep. Mike Snow addressed Sheriff Kellett after Ms. Taylor finished speaking to the panel.

"Sheriff Kellett, I can see here that you have some serious problems here in this county," he said.

Kellett agreed that Chattooga County has been bombarded with meth labs.

"We are getting as many of these labs as we can. But for everyone we bust, there's a lot more out there," he said.

CATHY BITTERMAN

Cathy Bitterman, state DFCS liaison to the GBI, said parents who are manufacturing meth in the presence of their children are literally putting a "loaded gun to their children's heads."

"These poor little ones play in the bi-products of meth and crawl on contaminated floors, touching objects used in meth production quite often," she said.

Bitterman added that when a fire or explosion happens where a meth lab is being processed, that the adult can and readily do run outside to save themselves.

"Their children are often burned and killed in these fires after being left behind by the parent," she said.

She added that most 'meth homes' offer hazardous living conditions to the children.

"There's almost always loaded weapons lying around close to the lab 'just in case,' she said.

DFCS, according to Ms. Bitterman, has been late in getting into the meth battle but is actively in the fight today.

"We have a new program called, 'Drugs Endanger Children's Program," she explained.

She said that the program, which had no state program, is working aggressively to educate public safety workers about children and meth labs.

She suggested that counties form a community meth task force to deal with all aspects of how meth is affecting children and other aspects of meth abuse.

"Children need more education in schools that is realistic about meth and we need to begin this education as early as kindergarten," she said.

If you have comments for Rep. Reece about the hearings or information relating to meth, you can reach her at 1-404-656-0305 or 862-2657.

Writers Comments: Additional stories about meth related topics can be found in "Meth Epidemic Targets Chattooga County," in this section.

Detective Jessee Hambrick Offers Advice

Det. Jessee Hambrick, Douglas County Meth Task Force, offered advice at a June 30 meeting on beginning a local drug task force in Chattooga County and surrounding areas. From left are Rep. Snow, Rep. Mosby, Rep. Barbara Reece, Hambrick and Gardner Sapp, a Georgia House research assistant. (Staff Photo by D. J. Laan).

Douglas County Begins Community Meth Task Force

By D. J. LAAN
Staff Writer

Jessee Hambrick, Douglas County Sheriff's Office, is a 10-year veteran narcotics officer. Rep. Reece, D-Menlo, asked Hambrick to address a Georgia House of Representatives Committee studying meth problems in Summerville last week about a new program started in Douglas.

"Officer Hambrick has some very special knowledge of all of this as well as facts about a new program started in his county that seems to be successful," Rep. Reece explained.

Hambrick said he and other Douglas County officers are seeing more young children on the streets using and selling meth these days than has ever been in his county.

"In the past, we would try to keep kids in sports or keep them busy with youth groups in churches and encourage parents to interact more with their children. None of that is working these days," he said, "where meth is concerned."

He said more young people are using meth in school as a first time drug choice.

Meth is being produced in all forms including one which is the size of an M & M candy and some of the new pills actually look like brown M & M's.

"Meth makes these kids feel great," he said.

LOCAL METH TASK FORCE

Officer Hambrick said his county initiated a new meth task force composed of community professionals and public safety employees.

"Members include people from law enforcement, fire departments and emergency services, the board of education, DFCS, local businesses, health providers and juvenile justice officials as well as other citizens," he explained.

He said the goal of the new "meth" group is four pronged: education, prevention, treatment and enforcement.

"You will be surprised to find out that many people have no idea what meth looks like, smells like — what it is," he added.

He said his county has also initiated a two-hour training session about meth for educators, which includes the Douglas County Board of Education and all teachers, paraprofessionals and those in related-education careers.

Officer Hambrick said new hires to the county's DFCS program receive training through the local meth task force.

"We have to educate early to prevent young people from getting on this drug," he said.

He suggested beginning education programs as early as three years old to offer them knowledge about how harmful meth and drugs can be.

Officer Hambrick said Douglas County is working very closely with Teen Challenge, a Christian behavioral program that treats young people who have meth and other addictions. He mentioned that other Christian groups are working in Douglas County to help those who use meth, also.

Betty and Jennifer Brady, Summerville and Officer Clint Young, Summerville Police Department, recently visited a Teen Challenge in Lithonia that is interested in opening a location that would serve Floyd and Chattooga County residents.

ENFORCEMENT

Jail and prison time is often a resolution to meth use but only if those sentenced have treatment programs available to them as part of incarceration.

"Just putting someone in jail doesn't mean you will stop them from being a meth addict. You might be for awhile but when they get out," he said, "then what?"

He said too many drug users are being sent to jail these days.

"If it keeps up as it is," he said, "we are going to run out of jail space."

Hambrick advocates treatment programs for first offenders.

He noted that the meth task force in Douglas County is bringing together a lot of smart folks with one goal in mind— eradicating meth from the county.

Jennifer Brady and Betty Brady, Summerville, will be working with Officer Hambrick in helping to organize a similar local meth task force in Chattooga County this fall.

To find out more on the Internet about Douglas County's innovative meth task force go to this website www. Meth-in-Douglas.com

Conference tackles meth 'epidemic'

07/01/04
By Diane Wagner, Rome News-Tribune Staff Writer
Respond to this story
Email this story to a friend

Clint Young, resource officer with the Summerville police, motions to different items that can be used to make methamphetamine during a Methamphetamine Study Committee meeting. Ryan Smith / RN-T

SUMMERVILLE — Nearly two-thirds of the 450 methamphetamine labs destroyed in the state last year were operating in Northwest Georgia.

"We're dealing not with a drug problem, but with an epidemic," said Pat Cook, a Walker County sheriff's detective assigned to the four-county Lookout Mountain Drug Task Force.

Cook, along with scores of law enforcement and social services workers, attended a conference in Summerville sponsored by the House Methamphetamine Study Committee on Wednesday.

The highly addictive drug — its street names include speed, crank, meth, chalk and ice — damages nerve cells over time and can cause paranoia, aggressiveness and hallucinations.

"I knew I was dying in a hurry," said Jennifer Brady of Chattooga County, one of the approximately 6 percent of methamphetamine addicts who manage to kick the habit.

But Cook said the effects of the drug go beyond the toll on addicts and their families.

The manufacturing process produces poisonous chemicals that permeate everything nearby, and they remain embedded until disposed of by a hazardous materials (Hazmat) team.

"As a general rule, the smallest meth lab in a cooler in the back of a car will cost taxpayers $3,000 to $5,000 to clean up," Cook said.

A serious health issue arises when the lab is in an apartment or rental house and the owner does not pay for the specialized cleaning before leasing the property to a new tenant.

46

One suggestion passed along to the House Study Committee was a law recently passed by LaFayette to combat the invisible blight. The local ordinance automatically cancels utility service and condemns residences where a controlled substance has been made. Reversal comes only after a certified hazardous materials cleanup.

"It will probably be challenged," Cook said. "But we've used it four times now, and owners of rental property are starting to police themselves."

Another suggestion involves stricter regulation of over-the-counter cold tablets, which are an essential ingredient in meth manufacturing. During its 2003 session, the Georgia General Assembly made it a felony to possess more than 300 tablets of ephedrine or pseudoephedrine, but law enforcers said retail sales should be limited to pharmacists.

Clint Young, resource officer for the Summerville Police Department, said all the other ingredients — such as matches, rubbing alcohol and salt — are readily available at stores.

"This is what we're up against," Young said. "Everything needed for meth is legal to have, legal to own."

Immediate treatment for first-time offenders, along with mandatory support-group sessions, is another key to slowing the epidemic, said Ann Davies, director of the Highland Rivers crisis stabilization programs in Dalton and Cedartown.

"There has to be follow-up; there has to be teeth," she said. "We've had success with support groups, but they won't come unless someone makes them."

Floyd County Commissioner John Mayes, who sits on the state Board of Corrections, said he came away from the conference with a deeper understanding of how pervasive the drug is.

"We need to be proactive about this," he said. "There is another perspective than just statistics."

State Rep. Barbara Massey Reece, D-Menlo, a member of the study committee, said four more conferences are planned in other parts of the state. A final report, with recommendations, will go to the Georgia General Assembly in January.

**Group Sessions Offered
For Recovery Drug Addiction**

A new Narcotics Anonymous (NA) group meets at 7 p.m. Tuesdays at Living Waters Ministries, off Ga. 100, in Summerville. The group addresses issues relating to recovery of those who have drug abuse problems. In addition, family members of those who do drugs are welcome to attend.

Jennifer Brady is the coordinator of the new group.

Everyday Ingredients Create Meth

Products found in most homes are used in creating methamphetamine. Items such as cold medicines, Red Devil lye and salt are just a few of the ingredients. (Contributed Photo).

The Summerville News

The Official Legal Organ of Chattooga County, Georgia

ummerville News   FEATURES AND NEWS

The Scourge Of Chattooga County: Meth
Whether You Call It Crank, Ice, Crystal, Glass Or Zip, It's Bad Stuff

Most Youth Protective Cases Related To Methamphetamines

Hooked On That Meth Feeling
Local Woman Hopes To Someday Be Drug-Free

Contributed Photo

The North Georgia Home Health Agency, an Amedisys company, decided they wanted to do something to help combat the drug problems in their local community, so they took action. They contacted their parent company and succeeded in securing a donation to help the local Chattooga County Citizens' Meth Task Force. Last Friday, March 4, Amedisys awarded Chattooga Family Connection a check for $1,000 on behalf of the Citizens' Meth Task Force. These funds will be used to continue community education through billboards, Meth educational brochure distribution, website information, and the continuation of the Meth Telephone Tip Help Line. Delivering the donation from Amedisys were employees Elaine Birge, Meca Underwood and Gail Weadon. Chattooga Family Connection members Susan Coalson, Meagan Goodman, Susan Stephens, Delight Pruitt, Michael Free, Mitch Williams, Chattooga Commissioner Mike Dawson, Ken Tribble, and Family Connection Coordinator Vicky Selman joined Meth Task Force Committee members Kaye Thomas, Betty Griffin, Linda Tinker, Betty Brady and Clint Young at the North Georgia Home Health office to tour their new facility and receive the welcomed donation.

ummerville News

FEATURES AND NEWS

Street-Smart Cop Is Meth Expert

Officer Works On Instincts and Street Savvy

Staff Photo by Jason Espy

OFFICER DAVID WESTBROOKS
With City Of Summerville Many Years

A Few Bucks For Ingredients Spawns Lots Of $$$$

Officer David Westbrooks, Summerville Police Department, said a $100 investment by a meth (methamphetamine) manufacturer can bring hundreds of dollars in return.

"Meth cookers usually manufacture the drug three times each week costing them around $300. After a year, the cooker has invested about $16,500 to manufacture meth. Considering that 167 people were arrested from Aug. 1, 2002 to present by the Chattooga County Sheriff's Office and 102 were arrested for possession, Westbrooks speculated that the arrests are small numbers compared to the use of methamphetamines in the county.

The money flowing through the community is in the hundreds of thousands of dollars from meth sales and it's staggering, according to the veteran police officer.

He added that many retail businesses in Chattooga County prosper because of methamphetamine manufacture.

Letters To The I

Wants More United
Effort Against Meth

Editor,

Hats off to your coverage of our county's drug problems. More and more, we hear horror stories of the death and despair of users and its toll on families. It seems to be getting worse, here and nationwide, and if it doesn't concern every parent and grandparent in Chattooga County, it should.

We read now of some law enforcement agencies which have specialized mobile "hose down" vehicles for on site treatment of children and other innocent victims exposed to meth during production, and our own Georgia legislature, backed by the Governor, has legislation pending which will allow criminal charges to be placed against anyone endangering children during this process. It seems we're slowly waking to the danger which has crept upon us.

All this is well and good, certainly on the right track. Another idea I would like to share or expand on is that of education to the general public as well as current users about the dangers, both physically and socially. I have sat in on a few of SPD Officer Clint Young's meth presentations and have observed that most of the honest and truly concerned general public is hungry for knowledge so that they can do a better job of protecting and preparing their loved ones for the inevitable... being offered meth. We are truly fortunate to have this program available, and we all owe "thanks" to our local Police Department for making it happen, and for the in-school program offered to children.

We know and hear of other programs being offered, from group to individual counseling, including in-house. We hear of recovering users (yes, it is possible) standing up and sharing their own painful experiences in an effort to help. We have educational books written by ex-users which allow insight into the mind of the habitual user. We are starting to see brochure displays in various places, spreading the word. We have various ministries addressing the matter. We have other projects being explored, all intended to get the attention of the user and help them see what they are doing to themselves and loved ones.

AS with any good effort, sharp criticism comes from those who need help but don't want it. No one is foolish enough to think all users can be helped. They can only be helped if they want help. Some are so far gone, or so totally selfish, their deluded mind won't let them care. It doesn't matter to them that lives are changed forever, that children are hurt or displaced, or that some grieving hearts may never mend. They can't recognize or tell the truth because they don't know what truth is anymore. These are the truly pathetic ones, and the ones I feel most sorry for.

The second group I feel sorry for are the ones who think their family is too socially prestigious to have this happen to them. Consequently, they spend time, energy and money on trying to hide the problem. It's time to wake up. Meth doesn't care who you are or who your daddy or mama is. Left unchecked, it will destroy anything it latches onto.

There are steps that can and are being taken by responsible citizens who love and care about our county. These are intended to strengthen us against meth. No one solution will do it, but dozens of individual efforts can bring results and payoff. Isn't this better than doing nothing at all? Ignoring meth won't make it go away. I would like to see more united effort, but even if that doesn't happen, small efforts can bring great rewards.

We all can contribute to making Chattooga County better, safer, and more drug free. I, for one, greatly appreciate the efforts of all those who do.

Betty Brady
Summerville

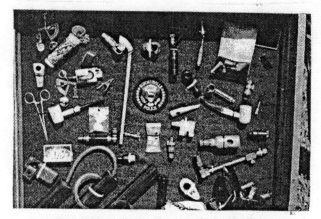

Drug Paraphernalia Legal In County

These items are examples of drug para-
phernalia confiscated by law enforcement
in Chattooga County. The sale of these
items is legal in the county as long as a sign
is posted by a retailer that the pipes will be
used for entertainment purposes only.
(Staff Photo).

Photo by Jessica Fleming

DO YOU READ THIS SIGN
Or Just Drive By Like So Many Others?

Most Youth Protective Cases Related To Methamphetamines

A front page story of July 25, 2003, in the Chattanooga Times Free Press by writer Ashley Heher said that the Tennessee Department of Family and Children's Services (TDFACS) has declared the use of methamphetamines as a regional epidemic where children are concerned.

Michael Miller, TDFACS commissioner, said, "Rehabilitating a meth family is not an easy task. It's a developing epidemic that we must get in front of now." He added that caseworkers in Tennessee are investigating between 72 to 90 abuse cases versus what the average caseload of a social worker might be – 52 cases. The News talked to Jean Hamilton, Chattooga County Department of Family and Children's Services (DFCS), Child Protective Services, who said that between 80 to 90 percent of her cases are related to meth use.

"I am afraid to see the long term health effects this is going to have on these kids who live in the environment of meth labs. I don't think anyone has actually studied that. I would say the statistics are not going to be good," she said.

Talking to Family Services in other areas of America, she said Georgia caseworkers often ask if methamphetamines are a problem in their areas.

"Overwhelmingly, we hear other agencies saying that the effects in their areas are devastating. About five percent of those who get treated can get off of it," she noted.

"These addictions are life altering. It looks so appealing in the beginning to them. Parents need to be aware of what is going on with their kids. A lot of younger people are involved in it," she said.

Hamilton said that there are some telltale signs of meth use that is usually present in all age groups.

"One of the signs is weight loss and the ability to stay awake days at a time," she said. She added that initially the young person will become very energetic.

"Chronic users get paranoid and often have little sores on their skin where they have scratched themselves. The user "tweaks" the skin thinking that there are bugs on their skin," she explained.

"I think Georgia DFCS agencies will be brainstorming and sharing of ideas on how to combat meth. We have the generations that are right now in our midst. We have to start with young people warning them about meth and keeping them from getting on the drug."

65 Of 70 Drug Cases Presented To Grand Jury Are About Meth

Officer David Westbrooks, Summerville Police Department, said this week that 70 drug cases have been prepared by the Chattooga County District Attorney's Office for presentment to the 2003 Grand Jury which is convening this week. Sixty-five of those cases are meth-related. Of the remaining five cases, one was a prescription fraud case, two were felony marijuana cases and two were cocaine-related cases.

Meth Task Force Is Forming In County

Sheriff Says He Wasn't Notified

By JASON ESPY
Staff Writer

"If they are not willing to jump onboard, then maybe someone will get elected that is willing," one man said about Chattooga County Sheriff Ralph Kellett's lack of participation.

Jesse Hambrick, of Douglas County's Meth Task Force came to Chattooga County to help form a local meth task force. But when he arrived Thursday night to speak, he found one key supporter in the drug war missing–Sheriff Kellett.

The Douglas County coordinator did not know that Sheriff Kellett was never invited. On Tuesday, Sheriff Kellett says he supports all aid in helping to fight the drug war but he was never informed about Tuesday's meeting.

"A task force brings everyone together," Hambrick said.

About 50 people from a wide range of backgrounds met at Mason Funeral Home's community room to discuss developing a countywide meth task force.

Those 50 included leaders from the Chamber of Commerce, health department, Lookout Mtn. Community Services Mental Health program, Summerville Police Department, Georgia Department of Juvenile Justice, a real estate agent, teacher, pastors and environmental hazard specialists to name a few.

"It's extremely important for the sheriff to participate. It's not necessary for him to attend the meetings, but he needs to at least send someone from his department that is willing to work," the meth task force man said. "This jurisdiction ranks third in the state for meth."

If this meth task force is successful, it will be the second in the state – Douglas County's was first.

Like Douglas County's that was created in February 2004, the purpose is to unite the community in an effort to combat meth and its production.

NINE STEPS

Hambrick gave nine steps that were needed to help Chattooga develop its own meth task force. Some of the ideas Chattooga's group of concerned citizens has already implemented.

Those suggestions include:
• Developing an anonymous telephone tip line. This will give citizens a chance to report any suspicious drug activity. "The Sheriff's department where I work gave us the phone lines to use. I mean they have several and we were given a couple regular lines. That's all you need. You don't need a 1-800 line," Hambrick said. The Douglas County man also suggests installing an answering machine.

• Develop a website. The website will educate the public as to what is happening with the meth war.

• Getting an e-mail address is important. This e-mail address should have the capabilities of being anonymous.

• Another suggestion was get T-shirts made with the county's meth task force logo.

• While the tee shirts may cost a little, Hambrick's next suggestion is free. Several national printing companies have published pamphlets and literature on meth use and its harm.

• The fifth suggestion Hambrick gave is already being implemented by the Summerville Police Department. Hambrick suggested hiring or appointing someone as a public speaker and coordinator for the meth problem. The Summerville Police appointed Officer Clint Young as its coordinator for the meth programs.

"You are already one step ahead of the game. You've got someone who'll get out and do public speaking" Hambrick said.

• The sixth step is retail training. This training will help clerks spot someone buying meth-related products.

• The seventh step is to advertise the meth group by getting

see METH TASK FORCE, page 8-A

from front page
a billboard. The county already has at least one billboard that is anti-meth. It says, "meth destroy. Jesus saves."

• The last suggestion was to use a four-prong attack to combat the meth problem. Those prongs are education, prevention, enforcement and treatment.

"A committee has been formed for each prong and each committee has a set of goals that is specific to their pronged approach . . ." Hambrick said.

For the treatment side Hambrick said, "The task force stands behind the theory that methamphetamine users and addicts need treatment."

"The education committee is geared toward those persons that are not at risk for methamphetamine use, but because of their work or personal involvement, need to be educated on what meth is and what dangers it poses."

What's Cooking In Your Neighborhood ???
Could It Be Methamphetamine ???

Some things to look for:
* Unusual, strong, odors (like cat urine, ether, ammonia, acetone, or other chemicals.
* Residences with windows blacked out.
* Renters who pay in cash. Most drug dealers deal in cash exclusively.
* Lots of traffic - Coming and going at all hours, especially at night.
* Excessive trash, including large amounts of antifreeze containers, lantern fuel, etc.
* Cans, red chemically stained coffee filters, drain cleaner and duct tape.
* Unusual amounts of clear glass containers being brought into the home.

Excessive amounts of the following items are suspicious....

Alcohol	Ether	Benzene
Freon	Chloroform	Paint Thinner/Toluene
Starting Fluid	Heet	Camp Stove Fuel
White Gas	Epsom Salts	Iodine,Black & Crystal
Battery Acid / Sulfuric Acid		Batteries/Lithium
Matches	Hot Plates	Cold Tablets
Drano	Diet Aids	Energy Boosters
Phenylpropanolamine		Phenyl-2-Propane
Red Phosphorous		Red Devil Lye
Propane Cylinders		Ephedrine
Bronchodilators		Rock Salt

If you suspect meth is being cooked, call our 24/7 Meth Hotline
578-2183
Chattooga County Citizen's Meth Task Force

#1 (Betty.psd)

proof is approved with no changes. If approved please FAX to (706) 354-0991.

uire another proof to show that changes have been made.

was created by Fairway Outdoor Advertising and cannot be used for any other purposes with out written permission from the General Manager.

t: .... Date: ....

FAIRWAY
Fairway Outdoor Advertising
www.FairwayOutdoor.com

Chattooga County Citizen's Meth Task Force

Mission Statement

The Chattooga County Citizen's Meth Task Force, begun in July 2004, was organized because we, the citizen's of Chattooga County, are concerned about the meth epidemic that is plaguing our community. We believe that our responsible citizen's owe it to our youth and general populace to make diligent effort to curb this plague.

We believe that most meth users were unaware of the dangers when they began usage, and that this lack of knowledge contributed to their bad judgement. We believe in the Christian principle of helping those who are in need, and are diligently seeking help for themselves.

We believe that education and knowledge are the key to prevention. We believe the combined, coordinated efforts of all our resources, including law enforcement and dedicated citizen's, can and will make a difference.

We believe our organized community "body" can give us a strong and viable voice which can effect legislation as needed, as well as seek assistance for projects which will enhance our basic goal, which is to help our county take a stronger stand against meth and it's devastating effects.

Our goal is to effectively pool and coordinate our efforts to encourage and aid our youth to resist drugs altogether and meth specifically, and to assist our local citizen's and law enforcement in making Chattooga County a better and safer place to live.

Chattooga County Citizen's Meth Task Force -- 4 major areas

TREATMENT COMMITTEE -- To be made up of several local treatment providers that offer a wide array of treatment options to those persons that desire to seek treatment. These programs consist of court mandated treatment both in custody and out as well as long term treatment for those seeking help on a voluntary basis. This enables those with a meth addiction to seek treatment before or even after law enforcement involvement and/or intervention has occurred. The Task Force stands behind the theory that methamphetamine users and addicts need treatment. These programs offer a wide range of program options for family members of those that are addicted to meth.

EDUCATION COMMITTEE -- Is geared toward educating those persons that are not at risk for Methamphetamine use, but because of their work or personal involvement, need to be educated on what Meth is and what dangers it poses. The Task Force will be involved with training efforts for DFACS workers, crisis shelter workers, public educators, fire department and / or law enforcement, and others who might request training on meth and meth labs. This training should consist of information that will help the student understand meth through its origins, appearance, and effects on the user as well as educate the student on how to identify a meth lab and how to respond to that discovery.

PREVENTION COMMITTEE -- Will focus their efforts on those persons who are at risk for Methamphetamine use. The committee is involved in obtaining, developing and distributing brochures and flyers on the effects of Meth and Meth labs. The prevention committee also acts as the public awareness arm of the Task Force and participates in local awareness through the Task Force website as well as being involved in local events and other functions that help raise awareness to what the Task Force is and has to offer.

ENFORCEMENT COMMITTEE -- Is geared toward the investigation and arrest of those persons that are involved in meth production or distribution. The Task Force website and tip line will be instrumental in offering local community members an avenue to report crime anonymously through the e mail system and phone hot line which will be monitored by the Task Force members. This information will be turned over to law enforcement to identify and arrest meth violators. The enforcement committee has a goal of strictly enforcing the drug laws that have been designed to

prosecute those that are involved in meth production and distribution.

The Chattoga County Citizen's Meth Task Force is moving forward in its fight against methamphetamine. Through community involvement, we can make a difference.

The e mail address is   chattoogacounty_methtaskforce@yahoo.com

Chattooga County Citizen's Meth Task Force
Hot Line Tip Report

Report Taken by:_____Date & Time _____
Suspect's Name_____Nickname_____
Suspect's Address or Location _____
Appx. Age_____Sex_____Race_____Hgt._____Wt._____
Auto Used_____Tag#_____State_____
Description of Vehicle_____
Location of Drug Activity_____
Description of Residence/Property_____
Is This A _____Building____Street_____Vehicle_____Other
Are there weapons____Handgun___Rifle____Shotgun___Other___
Are children present_____Guard Dogs_____Pets_____
Are lookouts present_____
What type(s) drugs_____Where_____
Time of Drug Activity_____Days_____Nights_____
Type of Activity _____Meth Manufacturing_____Illegal Grows
_____Drug Abuse_____Drug Trafficking
Drugs being sold or used ___Meth___Marijuana__PCP_____Crack
_____Cocaine _____Other
Additional Info or Comments_____
_____
_____
_____
_____

Informant's Name _____
Anonymous_____Phone#_____
E Mail_____Address_____
Willing to speak with an officer_____
Wish to be contacted by officer_____
Addt'l Info_____
_____
_____
_____

Report passed to_____Date & Time_____
Follow Up _____
_____

Meth Community Task Force Meeting Tonight

Citizens and officials interested in being a part of a Citizens Meth Task Force are encouraged to attend a meeting at 7 p.m. tonight, at Mason's Funeral Home in the community meeting hall.

Jennifer Brady, a volunteer, contacted Detective Jesse Hambrick, Douglas County, this week about assisting Chattooga County citizens in spearheading a local task force to assist law enforcement, community agencies and others interested in stopping a meth epidemic in Northwest Georgia. Douglas County has such a task force now, which is currently operating to wipe out meth in that county.

Anyone in law enforcement, education, public safety or health, business and concerned citizens are encouraged to attend.

In addition, several local citizens are interested in operating a 24-hour facility for persons who have a drug addiction such as meth. Betty Brady will report on what she has found out about some groups who have established successful centers. Anyone with ideas about such an operation or suggestion is asked to attend and participate.

A third aspect of the meeting will be to offer support to families with a loved one now using meth or trying to get off of the drug.

For additional details, contact Ms. Brady at 859-7875.

Menlo Council Hears Task Force
– See Page 3-A –

Menlo Council Listens To Meth Task Force

By DAWN
TREGLOWN WOOD
Staff Writer

Members of the Chattooga County Citizens Meth Task Force (CCCMTF) spoke at Tuesday's Menlo City Council meeting.

The task force members asked the Menlo Council to introduce and pass an ordinance in the city to control the access of products containing pseudoephedrine.

Pseudoephedrine is a product in many cold medicines and is used as a key ingredient to manufacture methamphetamine.

Chattooga County and Summerville have passed similar ordinances.

When questioned by council members about the progress of law enforcement in the war against meth, task force member and Summerville Police Resource Officer Clint Young replied, "We're doing what we can."

CCCMTF member and co-founder Betty Brady added, "if drug court would catch on, it would help the problem."

Brady referred to an 18-month drug rehabilitation program that has been established in other counties that's appeared successful in curbing drug use.

Since statewide anti-meth legislation would take months to write and pass the Legislature, and a drug court plan has not yet been established for the county, CCCMTF members urged passing of the ordinance to lessen meth manufacturing as much as possible.

Menlo Council members voted unanimously to table the ordinance until next month's meeting.

"This will give us the time to look over the ordinance," said Mayor Theresa Canada. "We're aware (meth) is a big problem for our whole county."

Canada said the proposed ordinance would affect about a half-dozen businesses within the city.

After the meeting, Brady said, "We feel optimistic about this."

OTHER BUSINESS

In other business, the council approved unanimously to fund the fire department's appreciation dinner at a cost of $400. The dinner is held annually, with no date set yet for the next one.

Council members also appointed and approved 2005 committee members.

Qualifying fees, which should be three-percent of member salaries for insurance purposes, were reduced because council members' salaries were reduced to help offset insurance and pension costs.

The qualifying fee for mayor dropped from $18 to $5. New qualifying fees for recorder and council members are $5 and 75 cents, respectively.

Newly-elected council members were also sworn in at the meeting. They were Virginia Tucker, T.J. Luther and new member Patricia Settoon, who took Virginia Welch's seat. Welch did not seek re-election.

At the end of the meeting, council member Eddie Majors commented that the city was having a problem with stray dogs. He said he would speak to the county commissioner about the problem.

"If the county doesn't do its job, it's not going to get paid," he said.

Menlo City Council meets again at 7 p.m. Tuesday, Feb. 2 at Menlo City Hall.

Address all mail to: THE SUMMERVILLE NEWS, P.O. BOX 310, SUMMERVILLE, GA 30747
TELEPHONE (706) 857-2494 • FAX (706) 857-2393

Thursday, January 6, 2005

Our Opinion

Meth Task Force Working Hard

The Chattooga County Meth Task Force has proved to be a strong proponent in the county to stem the flow of methemphetamine.

The group has tackled the meth problem with a vigor rarely seen in volunteer committees.

They mean business.

Not only will their efforts eventually reduce the numbers of people who may get on the drug, but their efforts will make the county a safer place.

The use of methemphetamine in Chattooga County is an epidemic. It is not only here that there is a huge problem — it is everywhere.

We commend the local meth task force for their hard work and hope they continue in the fight against the drug that has proven so devastating to so many children and families in Chattooga County.

Former Chattooga County Jim Parker signed a county meth ordinance before leaving office and that will help in the short term to curb the availability of meth-making pseudoephedrine. We hope the rest of the local municipalities will get on board and make the county solid in its efforts to try to curb the flow of the illegal drug.

Betty Brady

3-B
The Summerville News
Thurs., Jan. 6, 2005

Meth Task Force Fund-Raiser Set

By DAWN TREGLOWN WOOD
Staff Writer

The Chattooga County Citizens Meth Task Force (CCCMTF) will kick off a fundraiser during the last week of January to help offset the cost of billboards, said CCCMTF cofounder Betty Brady.

CCCMTF members are currently selling coupons for children's portraits, which will be taken the last week of January.

General Photographic Resources, based out of Cleveland, Tenn., is teaming up with CCCMTF to help raise money for the anti-meth campaign.

The meth task force has a billboard on Commerce Street, with less than two months left on the six-month contract.

A new canvas for the billboard will cost $550, and another six-month contract will cost $375 per month, or $2,250, for a total cost of $2,800, Brady said.

She said a new canvas would probably feature a four-year progression before-and-after photo of a meth user, which will have shock value and educate people to the reality of how drugs can affect a person's appearance. The new billboard would also have the meth task force's new telephone number and web site.

The fundraiser will consist of meth task force members selling portrait certificates for color portrait packages for children for $9.95, with the entire $9.95 going to the CCCMTF.

LIMIT

The certificates are limited to one per family and includes eight poses. If a family has more than one child, the first pose is a group shot of all of the children. The certificate is good for the first pose only and includes one 8 x 20, two 5 x 7's and eight wallet-size photographs.

Evening gown and tuxedo attire is provided for the children from three months to 10 years of age. Older children may be included in the portrait if they have a younger sibling 10 years old or younger in the photograph with them and if they bring their own appropriate clothing.

A portable studio will be set up the week of Jan. 24, at the Pentecostal Worship Center behind Reese's Tire Company on Lake Wanda Reita Road.

One week prior to that, appointment setters will contact the purchaser to set up an exact day and time for the portrait sitting.

Portraits will be available for viewing about two weeks after that, with additional portrait packages available for purchase.

To purchase a portrait certificate, contact members of the Chattooga County Citizens Meth Task Force at 578-2183, or call the marketing coordinator with General Photographic Resources, Sandy Marlin, at 822-0161.

Editorial LEAD 1/16/03

Drugs Continue To Be Problem

If you read the pages of The Summerville News then you should know that drugs continue to be a problem in Chattooga County and across the United States.
A youngster was caught with illicit drugs at Trion High School recently and methamphetamine labs have been destroyed all over the county. Drug arrests happen it seems every weekend on the roadways of the county and drugs proliferate everywhere it seems.
Drugs are not a black or a white issue. Drugs transcend race and gender and the destructive nature of drugs hits all the races, genders, socio-economic levels and everywhere in between.
The worst form of terrorism of all is in the form of drugs our young people take as well as every other age group.
Law enforcement personnel have a hard time keeping up with the number of people with drugs and with the amount of money involved, the dangers to the personnel increases. All they can do is stay vigilant and depend on law-abiding citizens to help them track down those who sell despair and death to our residents.
Drugs use is a dead-end street. Those that are afflicted don't realize it until it is too late.

The Summerville News
The Official Legal Organ of Chattooga County, Georgia

Editorial4 2-6-03

The Methamphetamine Epidemic

Methamphetamine in Chattooga County continue to be in epidemic proportion.
A number of methamphetamine labs have been confiscated in Chattooga County the past few weeks and the letup is nowhere in sight.
Methamphetamine is highly addictive, easy to get and reportedly easy to make. The only thing is when the labs are set up they are extremely dangerous because of the explosion possibilities and the poisons that are used to make methamphetamines.
Reducing the use of methamphetamine would be the ideal solution but it seems there is a market out there for the product. The next solution is a continued focus on arresting those that insist on breaking the law and put those responsible in prison.
Every time a methamphetamine lab is found in Chattooga County, the GBI has to call a company that contracts with the agency to clean up the chemicals because of the danger involved.
We commend the Summerville Police department and Chattooga County Sheriff's department for their hard work in catching those involved in these crimes.

Editorial2 7-10-03

Group Is Welcomed Addition

A Narcotics Anonymous® (NA) group will begin at 7 p.m. Tuesday in Summerville. The meetings will be held at Living Waters Ministries, off Ga. 100.
We wholeheartedly applaud the beginning of this valuable service to the people of Chattooga County.
We hope that people who want to get drugs off their backs and the backs of their families attend the meetings and begin their first step in overcoming their addiction.
The meetings are also for families of those on drugs to help them learn how to deal with their loved one.
We sincerely appreciate those that are beginning this tremendously valuable service. It is a testament of love for their fellow man.
The group will be a welcomed addition to Chattooga County.

Teaming Up Against Drugs

Members of the judicial courts and law enforcement, along with other concerned citizens of Chattooga County, stand among members of the County Drug Court in Alabama recently. Cherokee County officials shared information with the Chattooga County group about the operation of Drug Court system. (Staff Photo By Dawn Treglown Wood).

Local Citizens Observe Alabama Drug Court

By DAWN TREGLOWN WOOD
Staff Writer

State Court Judge Sam Finster sat on the other side of the judicial bench last Friday as he and almost a dozen other Chattooga County professionals observed proceedings in Cherokee County, Alabama's Drug Court.

Proponents for a drug court in Chattooga County were interested in the operation and proceedings of the system, and Cherokee County Drug Court officials welcomed the group into their courtroom.

DRUG COURT

Drug Court is an alternative judicial system of review, restitution, rehabilitation and sentencing offered to various criminal offenders. The system allows convicted criminals to have their cases transferred to Drug Court, where completion of an 18-month long drug and/or alcohol rehabilitation program allows participants the likelihood of case dismissals with sentences set aside.

The program helps free up costly court time while eliminating overcrowding in jails and prisons. Likewise, participants are offered important information, counseling and support to fight drug and/or alcohol addictions while dealing with issues and facing common problems associated with someone working and living outside the prison system.

Participants attend four phases of the program, with each phase addressing different issues surrounding drug use and rehabilitation. Each phase is 12 weeks long.

The first phase requires participants to attend court each week. During phase two that requirement drops to attendance bi-weekly.

The Drug Court in Cherokee County, Ala., currently serves about 400 clients.

PARTICIPANTS

Most participants of the Cherokee County Drug Court agree that the program can work.

One 28-year-old man, less than two months into the program, said he believes the program can help him fight a drug addiction, with the added benefit of keeping him out of jail.

"It keeps you out of jail for real, if you don't mess up," he said.

A 32-year-old man who was also sentenced to the same Drug Court said the program has taught him to deal with everyday issues.

"They give you plenty of rope to hang yourself, but if you're willing to work at it, it will work," he said.

People sentenced to drug court have certain criteria to follow which includes maintaining a job with no absences or tardiness, along with remaining drug-free – which is confirmed through sensitive, randomly conducted drug testing procedures.

Those convicted in Drug Court are given a color code. Each day a color is randomly drawn, and participants with that color code must submit to a drug test.

They are also assigned to support groups.

Both men agreed that one of the hardest things about the program is learning what it's like around-the-clock job, because run...

A Day In Court

Chattooga County visitors to Cherokee County, Ala.'s Drug Court listen as a judge explains how court will proceed. Judicial court and law enforcement attended the court proceedings along with attorneys, members of the Chattooga Citizens Meth Task Force and other concerned citizens. (Staff Photo By Dawn Wood).

One 28-year-old man, less than two months into the program, said he believes the program can help him fight a drug addiction, with the added benefit of keeping him out of jail.

"It keeps you out of jail for real, if you don't mess up," he said.

A 32-year-old man who was also sentenced in the same Drug Court said the program has taught him to deal with everyday issues.

"They give you plenty of rope to hang yourself, but if you're going to work at it, it will work," he said.

People sentenced to drug court have certain criteria to follow which includes maintaining a job with no absences or tardiness, along with remaining drug-free — which is confirmed through sensitive, randomly conducted drug testing procedures.

Those convicted in Drug Court are given a color code. Each day a color is randomly drawn, and participants with that color code must submit to a drug test.

They are also assigned to support groups.

Both men agreed that one of the hardest things about the program is keeping a job if it's a second shift job, because support meetings are during second shift. Phase 1 participants also must attend an hour-long support session six days per week.

VISITORS

Chattooga County visitors to the Cherokee County Drug Court proceedings last Friday were impressed with the court's success.

"I think this is great!" said Judge Sam Finster. "We need it in Chattooga County."

Assistant District Attorney Bruce Roberts and attorney Thompson said they were equally impressed and was appreciative that Cherokee County officials allowed the group to view the proceedings.

Judge Carver explained that the Cherokee County Drug Court does not accept cases from any individuals charged with trafficking drugs or manufacturing drugs or cases involving violence or use of a gun.

Likewise, she said she could sanction anyone sentenced in her court that violates any of the rules, including drug use. "Our testing is more sensitive than most," Judge Carver said. "They are also given a list of medications they cannot take if they test positive for drugs, they know they've violated the rules in some way."

BENEFITS

Though the Cherokee County Commission funded the initial $20,000 to set up the Drug Court, it is largely funded by public donations.

Judge Carver said her court is the only drug court program in the nation that is funded by public donations.

However, she added that the drug court has benefited the community in a number of ways.

Businesses want to hire the drug court participants, she said, because employers know the participants will not miss work or be tardy and will also be drug-free.

The program helps people fight drug addictions and keeps them in the workforce, so they can become respectable, beneficial members of the community.

Members of the Chattooga County Citizens Meth Task Force plan to inquire with several groups about available grants and other pertinent information needed to start and fund a drug court program in Chattooga County.

For further details, call 678-2183.

Judgment Day

Judge Sheri W. Carver presides over Cherokee County Drug Court in Alabama. The Cherokee County Drug Court is funded mostly through public donations. (Staff Photo By Dawn Treglown Wood).

Drug Court

The staff of the Cherokee County Drug Court in Alabama attends to 400 clients. Members of the court include, from the left, Deputy District Attorney Scott Lloyd, District Juvenile Courts Judge Sheri W. Carver, Drug Court Coordinator Vickie Moon, Certified Addiction Counselor Tammy Jackson, Drug Court Officer Joel Nowack and Drug Court Referral Officer Michael Terrell. (Staff Photo By Dawn Treglown Wood)

67

Editorial4 3-30-2003

One Death Is Too Many

It seems that legislators after almost every legislative session the last few years say they have toughened the state's driving under the influence (DUI) laws.
They have, however, it has not stopped people from driving while intoxicated.
In this week's edition of The Summerville News, five people were arrested during the week for DUI. Usually the numbers are between seven and 11. With numbers like that, it is just a matter of time before a tragedy strikes here and elsewhere across Georgia until a way is found to keep DUI drivers off the state's roadways.
One thought we hear is that taking driver's licenses away from offenders keeps them from working. Another argument is that they will drive anyway.
Whatever needs to be done, and the Georgia State Patrol, Chattooga County Sheriff's Dept., and police departments are doing their jobs -- a lot of people are being stopped and arrested for DUI, needs to be done in the legislature.
The legislature should take another hard look at what is happening on Georgia's roads. Drunk drivers are still there and the statistics in this county alone show there are a lot of them.
We wonder how many deaths of innocent people will be needed before a legitimate answer to the number of drunk drivers on our roads is addressed.
One death is too many.

The Summerville News

Edirtorial2 8--7-03   *The Official Legal Organ of Chattooga County, Georgia*

Meth Is A Death Trap

The Summerville News has run a two-part series on methamphetamine. The stories dealt with first-hand accounts of people who have suffered the hell of drug addiction. The stories point out the slow, consuming reality of methamphetamine addiction and what that addiction does to families and the people who are caught in its vise-like grip.
We talked with law enforcement officials who have to deal with the realities of meth use and meth labs. We learned what they look for and the despair they see when people are addicted.
Methamphetamine is a death trap.
Those that begin using meth innocently or naively don't see what is in store for them just around the corner. That is, until it is too late.
We urge parents to pay heed to any of the ingredients pictured in the article last week and if they find them around their kids. We urge all loved ones to watch for any tell-tale sign of use or addiction.
The greatest love a person can show is the care and concern when a loved one is either freed from drug use or helped to never begin.
When someone gives meth at a party of someone else. It is not because they are generous or nice, it is because they want to hook that person into addiction.
There is a unit of Narcotics Anonymous that meets on Tuesdays at Living Waters Ministry. It is open to those addicted as well as families who want to lean more to help their loved ones. The group is a community resource for help.
Methamphetamine is a community curse and it will take a community effort to rid our community of that curse.

The Catoosa County News

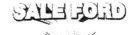

7243 Nashville Street, Ringgold, GA

Home

News

Sports

Funeral notices

Editorials/Opinion

Contact us

Photo galleries

Feedback

Order a photo

Entertainment

Guest Book

Contact your legislators

Calendar

Community

Classifieds

Subscriptions

Links

Calhoun Times

Cedartown Standard

Catoosa County News

Cherokee County Herald

Rockmart Journal

Rome News-Tribune

Walker County Messenger

Clear 38°F

by Intellicast Weather

Dissecting a drug epidemic

Officials discuss methamphetamine's social impact

CLICK

Chris Zelk

.. Methamphetamine is a social scourge that not only damages the user's body, but also impacts his or her family, employer and the community as a whole, a group of officials said on Wednesday at a seminar detailing the fight to rid North Georgia of the highly addictive drug.

The meeting, sponsored by the Catoosa County Chamber of Commerce, featured a wide array of health care and law enforcement personnel offering different perspectives on meth's impact on the community.

Terry Knighton, an addictive disease specialist with Lookout Community Services, on Wednesday discusses treatment options for methamphetamine addiction. (Catoosa News/Chris Zelk)

Chamber President Tammy Cole said she was surprised by the U.S. Department of Labor's recent estimate that the annual cost to American employers from on-the-job substance abuse is more than $100 billion. The USDL also estimates that 74 percent of illegal drug users are employed, and 10-20 percent of the nation's workers who die on the job test positive for alcohol and other drugs.

"The liability risk is very high," she said.

Detective Alan Miles, of the Catoosa County Sheriff's Department's narcotics divisio n, said he recently heard about an Indiana

Betty Brady

company that lost 52 percent of its employees to
meth addiction.

  "How would that affect Shaw Industries or an office
with three or four employees if they lost half of their
staff?" he said.

Detective Miles said that federal agencies conducted
controlled experiments creating meth labs in houses,
apartments and other settings to determine the extent of
contamination from meth production. They learned that during the
cooking process traces of meth cover virtually every surface inside
the building.

Tammy Cole

"That means that every toy, every bed sheet, every dish on the
counter is contaminated," he said. "So there is a huge danger
going into these places that we know now, but we're still
learning."

The labs and the d rug itself are created from common household
chemicals and utensils.

"If you give me a pocketknife and a roll of tape I can
probably go into 90 percent of the houses in this
county and have a meth lab up and running within
10 to 15 minutes," Miles said.

The detective describes the smell of cooking meth as   Steven Parlaky
"the odor of chlorine combined with iodine of tincture
and the nastiest pair of socks you've ever dealt with in your life."

A batch of meth can be made in two to 10 hours depending on the
recipe, Miles said. To compound the problem, cookers often teach
others how to cook, and an especially dirty form of the drug is
often smuggled in from Mexico.

Miles said that 80 percent of meth labs seized in the Southeast in
recent years were within an 80-mile radius of Chattanooga. He
said Catoosa authorities found 42 labs last year, and are already
on track to top that figure this year.

Authorities are now finding meth labs everywhere -- even in a
Whitfield County judge's office and "laying beside the road in a
ditch," Miles said. "It's here, and it's still coming."

Meth Survivor-Jennifer's Story

Roots of a menace

A German scientist first created meth in the 1800s.

Early in the last century the drug was legal in the U.S. and was prescribed for a number of ailments. A federal law enacted in 1970 restricted its use, and created a "demand vacuum," Miles said.

"That's when we started to see labs popping up in the U.S.," he said.

Japan, which has had its own meth problem for years, once permitted the drug's sale for dieters, Miles said, adding that Japanese kamikaze pilots in world War II often used meth.

"This is not just a United States problem," the detective said. "There are 12 to 15 other countries experiencing this epidemic."

The problem is symptomatic of Americans' tendency to self-medicate, Miles said.

"We don't deal with our problems," he said.

The drug, which comes in powder, rock and liquid form and is known by as many as 50 slang names including Crank and Ice, is favored because the high it produces lasts 10-12 hours, Miles said. Users become immersed in the culture of using the drug, he said.

Vanity is often the basis for meth use, with women being seven times as likely as men to use the drug in hopes of losing weight, said Catoosa Coroner Vanita Hullander, who heads the county's Meth Task Force.

"You're going to drop weight, but you're also going to drop your teeth, hair, everything," she said.

Dr. Steven Perlaky, an emergency room physician and director of emergency medical services for Hutcheson Medical Center, said the drug permanently damages the brain similar to Alzheimer's disease and dementia. It initially stimulates but then depletes the brain's supply of dopamine, which controls pleasure, Perlaky said.

Users eventually exhibit a variety of erratic behaviors, he said.

"They can be friendly one moment and angry the next, so it's a Jeckyl and Hyde situation," he said.

Users who can function on the job typically use small does, but "it'll catch up with them eventually," Perlaky said.

Betty Brady

Restricting ingredients

Detective Miles said that although a variety of chemicals can be used to cook meth, ephedrine or pseudoephedrine is the drug's base and must be included in the recipe.

State Rep. Jay Neal, R-LaFayette, said he spent more than 100 hours during the Georgia Legislature's 2005 session drafting House Bill 216, which places cold medicines containing pseudoephedrine behind store counters and limits purchases to no more than three packages.

Gov. Sonny Perdue signed the law, which goes into effect July 1, in a ceremony last week in Chickamauga. The law overrides all local ordinances.

"I believe this is a strong bill without being anti-consumer and anti-business," Rep. Neal said.

He said a component of the bill establishes a program called Georgia Methwatch, which provides free, voluntary training for retailers to help identify suspicious purchases.

Both Catoosa County Sheriff Phil Summers and detective Miles hailed HB 216 as a first step, but said that they would like to see Georgia pass stricter laws similar to legislation that Tennessee just passed, which places the cold medicines behind a pharmacist's counter.

"It is beneficial to law enforcement, but it's not what we need," Summers said. "We have a lot of businesses selling it out the backdoor. There's no question the system is failing."

Miles said that Tennessee is a model in dealing with the meth epidemic, citing the state's new law and a comprehensive Web site, which details the state's laws and local ordinances as well as education efforts and other resources.

"Tennessee is so far ahead that we're in the Dark Ages," he said. "Tennessee is third in the nation for lab seizures, but that is because they are actively seizing labs."

Financial, human costs

Sheriff Summers said the costs to provide medical care for county inmates who are addicts is staggering. He said that addicted inmates' medical care expenses increased by 300 percent for the same three-month period from 2002 to 2003.

Additionally, meth lab clean-up costs are high, and "we can't even use them as informants because we can't trust these people," Summers said. "They're unreliable.

"This is the worst drug that people are putting in their bodies," the sheriff said. "It's trash, it's poison."

Dr. Perlaky believes more emphasis should be placed on treatment and educating the public about meth's effects on the body.

"There has to be a better solution than what we're doing because clearly what we're doing isn't working," he said.

"Putting them in jail is not going to help," Coroner Hullander said. "When they get out they're still addicted."

Terry Knighton, an addictive disease specialist with Lookout Community Services, said that Northwest Georgia needs, but still does not have, a comprehensive detoxification program for meth addicts to get help.

He said he routinely sends patients as far away as Knoxville, Tenn., or Houston, Texas, for treatment because the metro

Betty Brady

Chattanooga area does not have a facility for users to detox from 21-28 days.

Similar facilities produced results in combating crack cocaine addiction in the mid-1980s, he said.

Knighton said there is also a list of between 40-60 people waiting to participate in out-of-state detoxification programs.

"That list is a death sentence," he said. "If you go back around this drug while waiting, you're going to use."

Knighton said a rule of thirds applies to meth addiction just as it does with any other disease. One third of users will recover, one third will relapse and start using again, and the final third will die from using.

He said that most meth users manage to function in society and often hold down jobs.

"That's important if you look at your perception of what an addict is," he said.

Knighton said the only available remedy for recovering meth addicts is a program of psychoactive drugs that curb addicts' cravings.

"Addiction lies in the thinking, not in the using," he said.

74

Editorial LEAD 1-4-04

Drugs Continue To Be Problem

If you read the pages of The Summerville News then you should know that drugs continue to be a problem in Chattooga County and across the United States.

Methamphetamine labs have been destroyed all over the county. Drug arrests happen it seems every weekend on the roadways of the county and drugs proliferate everywhere it seems.

Drugs are not a black or a white issue. Drugs transcend race and gender and the destructive nature of drugs hits all the races, genders, socio-economic levels and everywhere in between.

The worst form of terrorism of all is in the form of drugs our young people take as well as every other age group.

Law enforcement personnel have a hard time keeping up with the number of people with drugs and with the amount of money involved, the dangers to their personnel increases. All they can do is stay vigilant and depend on law-abiding citizens to help them track down those who sell despair and death to our residents.

A number of organizations have begun in the county such as Narcotics Anonymous and church-backed groups to help addicts and families of addicts. We salute the people who take their time in and effort to help those in Chattooga County gripped by the vise of drugs.

Drugs use is a dead-end street. Those that are afflicted don't realize it until it is too late.

The Summerville News

The Official Legal Organ of Chattooga County, Georgia

LEAD EDITORIAL 3-25-04

Proliferation Of Misery

It seems that every term of Chattooga County Superior Court and Sheriff's reports in The News that methamphetamine labs and people arrested for child abuse seems to grow.

The State of Georgia is considering tougher laws when meth labs are discovered and suspects are arrested. That is the only way that some of the labs will be stopped.

Heavy fines and mandatory prison time have been suggested for those convicted.

Methamphetamine is probably the number one drug problem in Chattooga County.

The dangers of people making the illegal drug with deadly chemicals are monumental. Special HazMat teams, in protective suits have to clean up the sites where the labs are found. Just think what that does to someone with no protection who is around while the drugs are cooking.

The State of Georgia is making it tough on parents that make meth with children in their homes. That legislation has been long overdue.

Even children have been encountered in the same home with a meth laboratory. Their lives have been jeopardized with the threat of an explosion or the chemicals themselves.

It's no wonder stronger sentences are needed.

We, like so many other Chattoogans, shudder when we read where a child has been abused. There is absolutely no excuse for the treatment some kids are exposed to in homes.

We agree that all suspects deserve a fair trial but we wonder about plea bargains and probation for those who maim and abuse children.

A recent child abuse case has drawn the attention of Chattoogans in its cruelty.

Law enforcement is doing a great job finding methamphetamine labs and making cases against those that abuse children. We just hope that those convicted are punished to the limits of the law.

Genes column 3-11-04

The Hobo

AN OLD HOBO was walking down the railroad tracks a number of years ago. People that saw him cowered away, not wanting to get close or maybe have him come up and ask for money. They were afraid.

The hobo took it in stride. He was used to the treatment of people that didn't look past his dirty clothes or his unkempt looks.

He was a very educated man and he often wrestled with the reasons he chose to live the life of a hobo. Maybe it was losing his wife and two children in a car wreck with a drunken driver. That sadness permeated every cell of his body and when the drunken driver went free with only probation – the hobo snapped or maybe the better way to look at it was he wizened up.

He enjoyed the lifestyle. The only problem he felt was there were fewer trains to hop so there were fewer destinations for him.

* * *

ONE EVENING IN A SMALL TOWN in Georgia, he camped out and was sitting, after eating supper, looking at the small fire he had built. He heard a rustle and saw a young teenager coming. The boy asked the hobo if he could sit down and talk with him for a short time.

The hobo was thrilled. He had little chance to talk with people, especially young people.

The hobo asked the young 13- or 14-year-old what he was doing out by himself.

"I have nowhere to go right now," the boy whose name was Tim answered. "My father and mother are arguing and they both are high on meth and grass."

The boy looked down at the fire.

The hobo told the boy that he was sorry.

"I understand your sorrow," the hobo said.

He proceeded to tell him of what had happened to him with the wreck and losing his family.

The boy looked up and said he was sorry.

"I guess my situation is not near as bad as yours, I feel so bad for you," the boy told the hobo.

The two went on talking for a long time and the hobo kept asking the boy didn't he need to go on home.

"No, they wouldn't miss me until tomorrow," the boy said. "Besides I feel good talking to you – you seem so smart."

"I've heard people talk about how dirty you are and how you look so messy in your clothes," the boy said.

"That doesn't bother me," the hobo said. "I learned a long time ago how important someone's heart and character is instead of looks. Besides, some of the absolutely best people I know dress hardly better than I do."

The boy was puzzled but was beginning to understand.

After a while of more talk, the boy said he had to leave.

"Be good," the hobo said, "study hard at school and make something out of yourself, because in the end it is yourself that really matters."

"Thanks, I will never forget you and what you have said," the boy said as he began walking away.

The hobo yelled as the boy got about 30 feet away.

"Remember one last thing, if you remember anything I have said," the hobo said. "I don't know where I read this or who wrote it but always remember, live while you have life to live and love while you have love to give."

The boy turned and walked into the night.

The Summerville News
The Official Legal Organ of Chattooga County, Georgia

1st Annual Chattooga
County Citizen's Meth Task Force Fund Raiser
"Cruise Against Meth"

Antique Car Show
Registration Fee
☆ **$20.00** ☆

Poker Run Registration Fee $20.00
Includes One Poker Hand

LIVE BANDS!
Tee Shirts for Sale!

Trophies For Best Car And Best Original Car!

$5.00 PER EXTRA POKER HAND
POKER HAND
1ST PRIZE $100.00
2ND PRIZE $50.00

HAMBURGERS , HOTDOGS & COLD DRINKS!

All Bikes Welcome!

Popcorn
Cotton Candy
And Cheesy Nacho's!

Bikes Out at 6.00pm

Dunking Tank!

Door Prizes!
Tickets 2/1.00

Horseshoe Tossing Tournament Registration Fee $10.00

August 26, 2005 @t Dowdy Park starting at 5.00pm

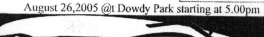

Jennifer Brady Speaks About Meth In Villa Rica

A local Summerville woman was invited to speak at an anti-meth seminar last Saturday at Ephesus Baptist Church in Villa Rica.

Jennifer Brady, a local recovering meth addict, was invited to give her testimony in a seminar dubbed "Celebrate Recovery." It was sponsored by Detective Jesse Hambrick Jr., of the Douglasville Sheriff's Department.

Several speakers, including Brady, of Summerville, were featured, giving testimonies as recovered methamphetamine users.

Jennifer and her mother, Betty, were among the invited speakers. Detective Hambrick introduced "The Power of Meth" a new book written by him, explaining meth and it's effects, mentally, physically, and psychologically.

JENNIFER BRADY

* * *

The Chattooga County Citizens' Meth Task Force will meet noon Monday at Pop's Buffet, downtown Summerville. The public is invited.

The Summerville News

The Official Legal Organ of Chattooga County, Georgia

Thursday, April 21, 2005

Our Opinion

Georgia Takes Huge Step

The State of Georgia took a huge step in the fight against methamphetamine this week when Governor Sonny Perdue signed a bill that will restrict access to the drug pseudoephedrine in cold medicines that is the main ingredient in methamphetamine.

Previously, Chattooga County, Summerville and Menlo took proactive stances in the fight against what is termed an epidemic in Northwest Georgia and all across the nation, especially in rural areas. A number of businesses in areas that did not pass the local ordinances also cooperated. Residents across Georgia appreciate their caring, progressive stance in doing what they could in fighting the problem.

The new state law will require retailers that sell any product containing pseudoephedrine as its main ingredient to place them behind the counter, as they do tobacco products.

The move is hoped to curb the rising meth abuse rate.

The state law also doesn't require medicine buyers to fill out information or when and where they bought the medicine.

Georgia Bureau of Investigation Director Vernon M. Keenan said the new law would help in the fight against "the fastest illegal drug in Georgia."

The idea behind the law is to restrict access for those that make methamphetamine to enough of the key ingredient so they can't make it.

We appreciate the Georgia Legislature in making this huge step and we, along with residents all over Georgia, hope it does the job.

We and all county residents appreciate Chattooga County, Summerville and Menlo and those businesses volunteering to put the pseudoephedrine behind their counters for their help in the fight against methamphetamine by passing and getting ready to pass similar ordinances earlier and helping in the fight against a drug that is so devastating to families and the community.

79

The Summerville News

The Official Legal Organ of Chattooga County, Georgia

Meth Law Will Aid In Fighting Drug

Methamphetamine use is the fastest growing drug threat in the United States. According to the 2002 National Survey on Drug Use and Health, 12.4 million U.S. residents over the age of 12 had used meth at least once in their lifetime. This is 5.3 percent of the population.

Meth has longer lasting effects than cocaine and is believed to be more quickly addictive. The recovery rate across the U.S. is 6 percent. This means out of 100 meth users, only six will be able to quit. The remaining 94 will eventually experience serious health problems with most dying within 10 years.

During the past year, Rep. Barbara Reece chaired a House Study Committee on the Dangers of Meth. This committee worked with other House Committees to pass legislation to address the growing meth problem in Georgia. "Health officials told us the drug has mostly been used by middle class, blue collar Caucasians, but is increasing in popularity with youth," Rep. Reece said.

"Our study committee was told that in one-third of the meth lab busts, there are children age 6 or younger in the household. Even worse, 10 percent of those charged with meth crimes learned to use meth from their parents. Our committee designed several bills which will further protect our children. These are in committee and will be considered next year," Rep. Reece said.

Increased methamphetamine use in Georgia has resulted in over crowded jails and prisons, huge backlogs of cases at the crime labs, and increased cases in the court system, according to Rep. Reece. A large number of bills designed to address various meth use problems were introduced in the legislature this year.

The House Judiciary Committee studied bills by Rep. Jay Neal, (R) LaFayette, Rep. Calvin Hill, (R) Woodstock and Rep. Barbara Reece. The committee chose Rep. Neal's bill, but many changes were made as the bill moved through committees in the House and Senate. The final version of HB 216 was approved by the legislature and signed into law by the Governor on April 19.

"Although this bill is expected to reduce the sale of pseudoephedrine products for illegal use, it is not as restrictive as my bill which would have required identification and a signed log which law enforcement could review," Rep. Reece said. "The Judiciary Committee heard testimony from many citizens who insisted that only a small percent of products purchased are used illegally. They said stricter control would make it difficult for the majority who purchase products for medical use," Rep. Reece said.

"The most important provision of the new law requires retailers to purchase products from a wholesaler licensed by the Georgia Board of Pharmacy. Law enforcement agencies will be able to review records of the wholesale business in order to determine suspicious activity," Rep. Reece said.

RETAIL

In addition, the new law requires retail stores to place sole active pseudoephedrine products (about 10 medications) behind a counter or barrier. A limit of three packages or nine grams may be sold.

The Georgia Meth Watch Program and the Georgia Council on Substance Abuse will provide training programs for retail business owners and employees to inform them of provisions of the new law. The law becomes effective July 1.

Some local governments already have ordinances which differ and in many cases are more restrictive than the new law. These local governments must change those ordinances to comply with the new statewide law by Jan. 1, 2006. (Rep. Barbara Reece may be reached at 706-862-2657 or the Atlanta office at 404-656-7859)

The Summerville Time
Thursday, August 25, 2005   7-A

A Force to be Reckoned with...

Betty Brady And The Chattooga County Citizens' Meth Task Force

By JESSICA FLEMING
Staff Writer

When Betty Brady joined the Citizens' Meth Task Force last year, she didn't quite know what to expect.

She was a mother, concerned about her daughter's struggle with methamphetamine and concerned about increased use of the drug in Chattooga County.

Today, one year later, she is receiving statewide recognition for her service to the community and battle against meth through the Citizens' Meth Task Force.

"We want to raise awareness first and foremost. The general public out there doesn't know what's going on — they don't have a clue. And, when you are uneducated about meth, you (can be) victimized by it."

Working in conjunction with the Summerville Police Department and various county governments, Brady hopes to develop a successful drug-prevention program in the near future.

"We've had so many people come and talk with us — so many people in this area have family members affected by the drug, so many have friends, neighbors," she said.

"There are more people touched by meth in this area than there are not (affected by the drug)."

Brady, however, hopes to see this trend disappear soon.

"We have some of the best law enforcement folks around, but they can't do it alone," she explained. "It's going to take a huge effort — more than small-town police officers. They say that (in Chattooga County) 1 in 3 people is directly affected by meth (either by being a user or having a family member addicted), and 1 in us housebolds in the county is manufacturing. We've just got to do something."

STATE-RECOGNITION

Brady was recently recognized by Governor Sonny Perdue for her fight against meth.

In early June she was inducted into the Georgia Commission on Women (GCW), a group of 15 women from across the state selected for their commitment and dedication to the education, welfare and empowerment of their community.

Brady attended her first official meeting of the commission Aug. 17.

"I primarily sat there and listened to what the other women had to say, to see what they are focusing on already

They have a huge project going on raising awareness of osteoporosis, which is fantastic. But in the future, I really hope to focus on Northwest Georgia's problems — drugs and everything associated with them," she said.

DRUG COURT

Indeed, one of the largest goals of Brady and the Citizens' Meth Task Force is to develop and implement a Drug Court.

"Statistics alone have shown that prison alone doesn't (fix) people addicted to meth," she explained.

She said that Drug Court is a way to save taxpayer money and clean up the county.

In addition to random drug tests, the offender is expected to maintain a steady job, attend counseling and pay all fines and fees associated with criminal activity.

"I think it will work because they will pay for their rehabilitation, rather than the taxpayers bearing the burden and paying for jail or rehab," Brady said.

She said there are several local judges and lawyers interested, but the Chattooga County Citizens' Meth Task Force doesn't presently have the funding to carry out their vision.

"We just don't have the funds together yet. It takes money to start something like this," Brady commented.

She hopes that her position on the GCW will lead to possible sources of funding.

"I'll be meeting soon with Thurbert Baker, the Georgia Attorney General. He has just given the GCW $50,000 to use in programs on health and nutrition across the state," she said hopefully.

Brady has selected 4 local individuals to attend this meeting with her this September as they campaign for Drug Court funding.

"I will be taking Kay Thomas, (Catoosa County's) Vanita Hullender, Sam Finster, and Stan Mosley.

"I feel that the five of us together, talking to the right people, can really accomplish something and let them know what's going on up here and what we need," she said.

Brady said that education is key to crippling the production of the deadly drug.

Brady hopes that GCW will provide opportunities for extending and developing the services of the Citizens' Task Force. She would even like to see a Governor's Meth Task Force eventually created.

"I told the GCW that I really appreciate the beauty of what they are doing (with women's health) and I can really see the beauty of what they are doing; but, I have my own agenda and I have a vision (of what we can do)."

"Parents have to talk to their children. The worst part about everything is that most people who get hooked on meth don't even know what they are doing. They don't know what they are messing with because they don't understand that once is all it takes."

With her new position on the GCW and great plans for the future of the Citizens' Meth Task Force, Brady hopes to not only save lives here in Chattooga County, but rebuild them.

UNITED AGAINST DRUGS

Several local law enforcement officials attended last Thursday's anti-meth law meeting in Ft. Oglethorpe, organized by State Sen. Jeff Mullis and Representative-elect Jay Neal. From left are Sen. Mullis, Chattooga County Sheriff Ralph Kellett, Rep.-elect Neal, Chattooga County Resource Officer Clint Young, Trion Police Officer Chris Harris and Trion Police Chief Charles Latta. (Staff Photo By Dawn Treglown Wood).

FIGHTING THE WAR ON DRUGS

Local law enforcement officials, legislators and concerned citizens attended last Thursday's meeting in Ft. Oglethorpe to discuss a proposed statewide anti-meth law. From left are Chattooga County retired businessman Boyce Dooley, Chattooga County Citizens Meth Task Force co-founder Betty Brady, Chattooga County Citizens Meth Task Force co-founder Jennifer Brady, Chattooga County Sheriff Ralph Kellett, Chattooga County Chief Deputy Eddie Colbert, Senator Jeff Mullis, Representative-elect Jay Neal, Trion Police Chief Charles Latta, Trion Police Officer Chris Harris and Summerville Police Resource Officer Clint Young. (Staff Photo By Dawn Treglown Wood).

The Summerville News

Thursday, January 6, 2005

Senator Jeff Mullis, Rep
Enforcement Discuss St

FEATURES AND NEWS

-B

.-Elect Neal, Local Law
atewide Anti-Meth Bill

IRONING OUT THE DETAILS

Many details of the anti-meth law still need to be ironed out before it is introduced in the legislature, and Sen. Mullis asked that the officers discuss proposed issues with their respective departments. He hopes that the group can meet on a quarterly basis until all details of the bill are worked out and the bill can be introduced. Even then, it would be a while before the proposed bill became law, since it must pass through both the House of Representatives and the Senate for approval before it is signed into law.

"Sen. Mullis has been a strong supporter of the GBI," said GBI Director Vernon Keenan. "We'll be working closely with him to perfect legislation regarding the meth crisis in Georgia."

Meanwhile, local governments can help by passing ordinances for restriction of the products.

Summerville and Chattooga County have an ordinance in place, and Betty Brady and other members of the Chattooga County Citizens Meth Task Force hopes to persuade the Menlo City Council and the Lyerly City Council to introduce and approve similar ordinances.

DRUG COURT

Also, implementation of a drug court, which is a court-ordered drug rehabilitation program, would help ease

COMING TOGETHER

From left, Chattooga County Sheriff Ralph Kellett, Walker County Sheriff Steve Wilson and Catoosa County Sheriff Phil Summers discuss the severity of the meth problems surrounding Northwest Georgia. The sheriffs offered their opinions of a proposed statewide anti-meth law at last Thursday's meeting in Ft. Oglethorpe. (Staff Photo By Dawn Treglown Wood).

overcrowding of prisons while helping those addicted to meth that are not violent criminals or hardcore users or manufacturers of the drug.

DeKalb County, Ala., officials have implemented a drug court in that jurisdiction that has not only reduced the number of meth arrests but has also had a high success rate for rehabilitation of meth users.

"I think it would be very beneficial for Chattooga County," said Sen. Mullis.

DeKalb County was donated a 1,500-square-feet building for its facility and renovated it with $10,000 in donations.

Sen. Mullis said that

Chattooga County has a lot of families dealing with the meth crisis that would see a drug court as something this useful for the county.

"Chattooga County has a lot of concerned and caring people," he said.

For details, contact the Chattooga County Citizens Meth Task Force at 578-2183.

Enforcement Discuss Sta

By DAWN
TREGLOWN WOOD
Staff Writer

Senator Jeff Mullis and Representative-elect Jay Neal met with local law enforcement officials last Thursday in Fort Oglethorpe to discuss details for a proposed statewide bill to regulate ingredients used to manufacture methamphetamine.

Methamphetamine is a dangerous drug and its use has increased rapidly throughout the country, especially in Northwest Georgia. The drug can cause permanent brain damage, hallucinations, extreme paranoia, various health problems and even death.

Because meth destroys synapses or connections between brain cells, up to 18 months are required to abstain from using the drug once a use of habit has been established — which is usually very quickly, within three times of use.

MAKING PROGRESS

From left, Representative-elect Jay Neal and Senator Jeff Mullis discuss the progress being made to introduce legislation for a statewide anti-meth law. A meeting in Ft. Oglethorpe last Thursday brought together law enforcement officials to discuss details of the proposed law. (Staff Photo By Dawn Treglown Wood).

PSEUDOEPHEDRINE RESTRICTIONS

Meth is made using dangerous chemicals including lye and battery acid. A key ingredient of the manufacturing process is ephedrine or pseudoephedrine. Many common cold medicines contain pseudoephedrine and are used in large quantities by meth "cookers."

Stricter control of the products that contain ephedrine or pseudoephedrine would decrease meth production. This was the case in Oklahoma, where meth production was significantly curbed after state legislation passed which restricted the availability of products containing ephedrine or pseudoephedrine.

The Summerville City Council recently approved an ordinance, effective Feb. 1, which will require that any product containing ephedrine or pseudoephedrine will be placed behind the counter and require a picture ID and signature for purchase.

The Floyd County Council also approved a similar ordinance last week, which went into effect Jan. 1. However, that ordinance is not enforceable within the county's municipalities of Rome and Cave Spring. Floyd County's ordinance also restricted those products containing more than 25 mg. of ephedrine or pseudoephedrine and excludes gel caps, time-release products and liquids.

"If it's got pseudoephedrine in it, you can make meth with it," said Ft. Oglethorpe Police Detective Ira Taylor.

Detective Taylor conducts meth workshops in Northwest Georgia along with a fellow officer, Detective Rick Posey. They conducted more than 200 of the informative workshops last year, speaking to teachers, emergency medical technicians and any other groups that requested them.

LAW ENFORCEMENT INPUT

Sen. Mullis had the legislative council draw up a preliminary senate bill, which was offered to local law enforcement officials for discussion of exclusions or inclusions that would make the statewide bill effective.

Sen. Mullis and Rep.-elect Neal gathered with officials from the Georgia Bureau of Investigation (GBI) along with sheriffs, detectives and investigators from counties throughout Northwest Georgia to go over the proposed bill.

Several concerned citizens that are proponents for a statewide meth bill were also invited to the meeting.

Attending from Chattooga County were Chattooga County Sheriff Ralph Kellett, Summerville Police Resource Officer Clint Young and the Chattooga County Citizens Meth Task Force co-founders

METH EDUCATION

Ft. Oglethorpe Police Detective Ira Taylor answers questions about meth production at last Thursday's meeting of legislators and law enforcement officials. Taylor helps conduct meth workshops to educate the public about the dangers of methamphetamine use and manufacturing. (Staff Photo By Dawn Treglown Wood).

Betty Brady and Jennifer Brady.

Rep.-elect Neal told the law enforcement officials, "We are trying to get legislation in that will make your efforts more effective."

He said that law enforcement could help with the specifics of the bill, because it's the law enforcement officers that are on the streets, dealing with the manufacturers of meth. They would know what would be most effective.

"The meth crisis extends far beyond being a user of the drug," said Rep.-elect Neal. "The dangerous process of manufacturing meth puts families in harm's way in more ways than one. All too often, a child is forced into foster care or becomes a ward of the state because their mother or father has been incarcerated for using or producing the drug. More and more, our county governments are put under financial pressure to jail and provide healthcare for those addicted to meth. We have to do something to try to get this emergency under control, and I am willing to do anything I can to help."

Sen. Mullis agreed.

"Methamphetamine is at a crisis level in the state of Georgia, but in Northwest Georgia, the meth problem is an epidemic. It is crucial that we do something to slow down this problem and do all we can to eliminate it from our communities," Sen. Mullis said. "I appreciate the help from local and state law enforcement as I research and write this legislation."

PROPOSED LEGISLATION

A pertinent piece of the proposed legislation will require that ephedrine or pseudoephedrine products be placed behind the counter in stores. The belief is that restriction of the availability of the products used to manufacture meth will curb the problem in the early stages of manufacturing.

The proposed bill includes a provision to keep the product behind the counters of pharmacies only, not convenient stores and other locales.

Although Sen. Mullis thought some of the officials might oppose that portion, all of them seemed to approve of it. Many of them agreed that some storeowners are not keeping effective records of inventories and receipts.

One official cited evidence that flats of medicine have been sold out the back doors of some convenient stores. The group agreed that someone certified by the State Board of Pharmacy would be more likely to keep efficient records of the purchasing and selling of ephedrine and pseudoephedrine products.

The proposed anti-meth bill would also strengthen state conspiracy laws to allow law enforcement to crack down on any individual or business selling excessive amounts of those products.

Restricting access to a dwelling that is contaminated by meth production was also addressed, along with contamination of vehicles.

Although details for that provision will be discussed further, many agreed that a letter informing of meth contamination should be attached to a property deed or registered with the tax office and not removed until contamination is eliminated.

"I greatly appreciate what Sen. Mullis and Rep.-elect Neal are doing," said Pat Stanfield, Commander of the Lookout Mountain Judicial Drug Task Force. "This legislation will be helpful in fighting meth and protecting innocent citizens that unknowingly move into properties that have previously been contaminated."

Clean-up costs were also discussed, with the possibility of placing that responsibility in the hands of the Department of Natural Resources (DNR).

County Meth Ordinance Signed By Commissioner

Will Restrict Access To Ephedrine, Pseudoephedrine

By JASON ESPY
Staff Writer

Those making methamphetamine will find it harder to get the key ingredients as more local governments adopt laws limiting the sale of certain items. Chattooga County joined the list adopting an ordinance Friday.

Cold medicines such as, Comtrex, Dimetapp, Theraflu and Tylenol Sinus, will be harder to obtain if new laws are adopted. These products contain the key ingredient for meth, ephedrine and pseudoephedrine.

"Products used in the preparation of methamphetamine may not be openly displayed for sale in Chattooga County, but must be maintained behind the counter and distributed for sale only by the pharmacist, pharmacy technician, sales clerk or other retail distributor employee," according to the county's proposed ordinance.

The City of Summerville was the first to tackle the meth ordinance. Since then, Floyd County has restricted the products. Council members from the Town of Trion and Menlo also have expressed interest in enacting the law.

PHOTO ID

If adopted, the ordinance mandates that customers bring photo identification and a sign a logbook. Storeowners must keep that logbook for at least three years, according to the proposed county ordinance.

". . . (People) to produce a photo identification showing their date of birth and sign a written log or receipt showing their signature and printed name, the date of the transaction, the type and amount of product purchased and consent to said information being distributed to law enforcement personnel," the ordinance states.

Businesses violating this ordinance will be punished by a $500 fine per occurrence, the ordinance states.

"Products used in the preparation of methamphetamine may not be openly displayed for sale in Chattooga County, but must be maintained behind the counter and distributed for sale only by the pharmacists, pharmacy technician, sales clerk or other retail distributor employee," the proposed ordinance states.

The ordinance was signed by outgoing Sole County Commissioner Jim Parker on his last day in office.

Law enforcement officials believe this law will make it harder for criminals to get these cold medicines in bulk quantities.

Although it may be harder to obtain, officers admit it won't be impossible. This is especially true if other neighboring counties and states don't pass similar ordinances.

The city's ordinance effective date is Feb. 1. The county's effective date will also be the same if fully enacted.

Betty Brady

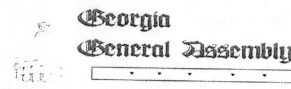

Georgia
General Assembly

05 HB 216/AP
House Bill 216 (AS PASSED HOUSE AND SENATE)
By: Representatives Neal of the 1st, Ralston of the 7th, Miller of the 106th, Burmeister of the 119th, Sheldon of the 105th, and others

A BILL TO BE ENTITLED
AN ACT

To amend Chapter 13 of Title 16 of the Official Code of Georgia Annotated, relating to controlled substances, so as to limit the sale and manner of sale of products containing pseudoephedrine; to provide for exceptions; to provide for mitigation of punishment under certain circumstances; to provide for penalties; to restrict the sale, transfer, manufacture, purchase for resale, and furnishing of certain substances; to provide for definitions; to authorize the State Board of Pharmacy to promulgate certain rules and regulations; to provide for licensing and permitting of persons who sell, transfer, purchase for resale, or otherwise furnish or possess certain chemicals; to require certain records to be maintained; to provide for exceptions; to provide for certain forfeitures; to provide for penalties; to provide for certain reports; to provide that it is illegal for a person to possess any substance with the intent to use such substance in the manufacture of a Schedule I or Schedule II controlled substance or to knowingly convey such substance to another for use in the manufacture of a Schedule I or Schedule II controlled substance; to provide for certain considerations with regard to determining whether such substances were possessed illegally; to provide for exceptions; to provide for penalties; to provide for related matters; to provide an effective date; to repeal conflicting laws; and for other purposes.

BE IT ENACTED BY THE GENERAL ASSEMBLY OF GEORGIA:

SECTION 1.

Chapter 13 of Title 16 of the Official Code of Georgia Annotated, relating to controlled substances, is amended by adding a new subsection (b.1) to Code Section 16-13-30.3, relating to possession of substances containing ephedrine, pseudoephedrine, and phenylpropanolamine, to read as follows:

.(b.1)(1) Products whose sole active ingredient is pseudoephedrine may be offered for retail sale only if sold in blister packaging. Such products may not be offered for retail sale by self-service, but only from behind a counter or other barrier so that such products are not directly accessible by the public but only by a retail store employee or agent.
(2) No person shall deliver in any single over the counter sale more than three packages of any product containing pseudoephedrine as the sole active ingredient or in combination with

other active ingredients or any number of packages that contain a combined total of more than nine grams of pseudoephedrine or its base, salts, optical isomers, or salts of its optical isomers.

(3) It shall be unlawful for a retail distributor to purchase any product containing pseudoephedrine from any person or entity other than a manufacturer or a wholesale distributor licensed by the Georgia Board of Pharmacy.

(4) This subsection shall not apply to:

  (A) Pediatric products labeled pursuant to federal regulation as primarily intended for administration to children under 12 years of age according to label instructions; and

  (B) Products that the Georgia Board of Pharmacy, upon application of a manufacturer, exempts because the product is formulated in such a way as to effectively prevent the conversion of the active ingredient into methamphetamine or its salts or precursors.

(5) This subsection shall preempt all local ordinances or regulations governing the retail sale of over the counter products containing pseudoephedrine by a retail business except such local ordinances or regulations that existed on or before December 31, 2004. Effective January 1, 2006 the subsection shall preempt all local ordinances.

(6)(A) Except as otherwise provided herein, it shall be unlawful for any person knowingly to violate any prohibition contained in paragraph (1), (2), or (3) of this subsection.

(B) Any person convicted of a violation of paragraph (1) or (2) of this subsection shall be guilty of a misdemeanor which, upon the first conviction, shall be punished by a fine of not more than $500.00, and, upon the second or subsequent conviction, shall be punished by not more than six months imprisonment or a fine of not more than $1,000.00, or both.

(C) Any person convicted of a violation of paragraph (3) of this subsection shall, upon the first conviction, be guilty of a misdemeanor and, upon the second or subsequent conviction, be guilty of a misdemeanor of a high and aggravated nature.

(D) It shall be a defense to a prosecution of a retail business or owner or operator thereof for violation of paragraph (1) or (2) of this subsection that, at the time of the alleged violation, all of the employees of the retail business had completed training under Georgia Meth Watch, the retail business was in compliance with Georgia Meth Watch, and the defendant did not knowingly, willfully, or intentionally violate paragraph (1) or (2) of this subsection. For purposes of this subsection only, the term 'Georgia Meth Watch' shall mean that program entitled 'Georgia Meth Watch' or similar program which has been promulgated, approved, and distributed by the Georgia Council on Substance Abuse.

(7) Except as otherwise provided in this subsection, the State Board of Pharmacy may adopt reasonable rules and regulations to effectuate the provisions of this subsection. The board is further authorized to charge reasonable fees to defray expenses incurred in maintaining any records or forms necessitated by this subsection or otherwise administering any other provisions of this subsection..

SECTION 2.

Said chapter is further amended by adding a new Code Section 16-13-30.4 to read as follows:

.16-13-30.4.

(a) As used in this Code section and unless otherwise specified, the term 'board' or 'Board of Pharmacy' shall mean the Georgia State Board of Pharmacy.

(b)(1) A wholesale distributor who sells, transfers, purchases for resale, or otherwise furnishes any product containing pseudoephedrine must first obtain a license from the Board of Pharmacy; provided, however, that a wholesale distributor that has a valid license as a

4/22/2005

wholesale distributor under Code Section 26-4-113 shall not be required to obtain an additional license under this Code section.

(2) Wholesale distributors licensed under Code Section 26-4-113 shall be subject to the provisions of this Code section in the same manner as wholesale distributors licensed under this Code section.

(3) Every wholesale distributor licensed as provided in this Code section shall:

(A) Submit reports, upon verbal or written request from the Georgia Drugs and Narcotics Agency, the Georgia Bureau of Investigation, or the sheriff of a county or the police chief of a municipality located in this state, to account for all transactions with persons or firms located within this state; such reportable transactions shall include all sales, distribution, or transactions dealing with products containing pseudoephedrine; and

(B) Within seven days, notify the Georgia Drugs and Narcotics Agency of any purchases of products containing pseudoephedrine from the wholesale distributor which the wholesaler judges to be excessive.

(4) Whenever any firm or person located in this state receives, purchases, or otherwise gains access to products containing pseudoephedrine from any wholesale distributor, whether located in or outside this state, such firm or person shall maintain a copy of such wholesale distributor's license issued by the Georgia State Board of Pharmacy. Such firm or person shall maintain copies of all invoices, receipts, and other records regarding such products containing pseudoephedrine for a minimum of three years from the date of receipt, purchase, or access. Failure to maintain records to verify the presence of any and all products containing pseudoephedrine being held by a firm or person shall subject such products containing pseudoephedrine to being embargoed or seized by proper law enforcement authorities until such time as proof can be shown that such products containing pseudoephedrine were obtained from a Georgia licensed wholesale distributor.

(5) Agents of the Georgia Drugs and Narcotics Agency, agents of the Georgia Bureau of Investigation, and the sheriff of a county or the police chief of a county or municipality in this state in which a firm or person that receives, purchases, or otherwise gains access to products containing pseudoephedrine is located may request to review the receiving records for such products. Failure to provide such records within five business days following such request to account for the presence of such products shall result in the embargo or seizure of such products.

(c) A license or permit obtained pursuant to this Code section shall be denied, suspended, or revoked by the Board of Pharmacy upon finding that the licensee or permit holder has:

(1) Furnished false or fraudulent material information in any application filed under this Code section;

(2) Been convicted of a crime under any state or federal law relating to any controlled substance;

(3) Had his or her federal registration suspended or revoked to manufacture, distribute, or dispense controlled substances;

(4) Violated the provisions of Chapter 4 of Title 26; or

(5) Failed to maintain effective controls against the diversion of products containing pseudoephedrine to unauthorized persons or entities.

(d) The Board of Pharmacy may adopt reasonable rules and regulations to effectuate the provisions of this Code section. The board is further authorized to charge reasonable fees to defray expenses incurred in issuing any licenses or permits, maintaining any records or forms required by this Code section, and the administration of the provisions of this Code section.

(e) Notwithstanding any other provision of this Code section to the contrary, no person shall be required to obtain a license or permit for the sale, receipt, transfer, or possession of a product containing pseudoephedrine when:

(1) Such lawful distribution takes place in the usual course of business between agents or employees of a single regulated person or entity; or

(2) A product containing pseudoephedrine is delivered to or by a common or contract carrier for carriage in the lawful and usual course of the business of the common or contract carrier or to or by a warehouseman for storage in the lawful and usual course of the business of the warehouseman.

(f) All products containing pseudoephedrine that have been or that are intended to be sold, transferred, purchased for resale, possessed, or otherwise transferred in violation of a provision of this Code section shall be subject to forfeiture to the state and no property right shall exist in them.

(g)(1) Any person who sells, transfers, receives, or possesses a product containing pseudoephedrine violates this Code section if the person:

(A) Knowingly fails to comply with the reporting requirements of this Code section;

(B) Knowingly makes a false statement in a report or record required by this Code section or the rules adopted thereunder; or

(C) Is required by this Code section to have a license or permit and knowingly or deliberately fails to obtain such a license or permit.

(2) It shall be illegal for a person to possess, sell, transfer, or otherwise furnish a product containing pseudoephedrine if such person possesses, sells, transfers, or furnishes the substance with the knowledge or intent that the substance will be used in the unlawful manufacture of a controlled substance.

(3)(A) A person who violates paragraph (2) of this subsection shall be guilty of a felony and, upon conviction thereof, shall be punished by imprisonment for not less than one nor more than 15 years or by a fine not to exceed $100,000.00, or both.

(B) A person who violates any provision of this Code Section other than paragraph (2) of this subsection shall be guilty of a misdemeanor on the first offense and a misdemeanor of a high and aggravated nature on the second and subsequent offenses..

SECTION 3.

Said chapter is further amended by adding a new Code Section 16-13-30.5 to read as follows:

.16-13-30.5.

(a) It shall be illegal for a person to possess, whether acquired through theft or other means, any substance with the intent to:

(1) Use such substance in the manufacture of a Schedule I or Schedule II controlled substance; or

(2) Knowingly convey such substance to another for use in the manufacture of a Schedule I or Schedule II controlled substance.

(b) In determining whether a particular substance is possessed with the intent required to violate subsection (a) of this Code section, the court or other authority making such a determination may, in addition to all other logically relevant factors, consider the following:

(1) Statements by the owner or anyone in control of the substances concerning its use;

(2) Prior convictions, if any, of the owner or of anyone in control of the substances for violation of any state or federal law relating to the sale or manufacture of controlled substances;

(3) Instructions or descriptive materials of any kind accompanying the substance or found in the owners or controlling persons possession concerning, explaining, or depicting its use;
(4) The manner in which the substance is displayed or offered for sale;
(5) The quantity and location of the substance considered in relation to the existence and scope of legitimate uses for the substance in the community; and
(6) Expert testimony concerning the substances use.
(c) This Code section shall not apply where possession was by a person authorized by law to dispense, prescribe, manufacture, or possess the substance in question.
(d) A person who violates this Code section shall be guilty of a felony and, upon conviction thereof, shall be punished by imprisonment for not less than one nor more than fifteen years or by a fine not to exceed $100,000.00, or both..

SECTION 4.
This Act shall become effective on July 1, 2005.

SECTION 5.
All laws and parts of laws in conflict with this Act are repealed.
□

Walker County Messenger

136 E. Patton Street, LaFayette, GA

638-0095

Home
News
Sports
Funeral notices
Community calendar
Editorials & opinion
Society & lifestyles
Contact us
Photo galleries
Order a photo
Message board
Feedback
About us
Entertainment
Guest book
Contact your legislators
Subscriptions
Advertising
Classifieds
Links
Calhoun Times
Catoosa County News
Cedartown Standard
Cherokee County Herald
Rockmart Journal
Rome News-Tribune

Governor comes to Walker to sign meth legislation

Tim Carlfeldt

... More than 100 people greeted Gov. Sonny Perdue Tuesday in Chickamauga to witness the signing of a statewide anti-meth measure.

Gov. Sonny Perdue puts on his jacket after safely landing from a helicopter on a clearing next to the Food Lion in Chickamauga Tuesday afternoon. (Messenger photo/Ken Caruthers)

The governor arrived by helicopter at the Food Lion on U.S. 27 for a ceremony to give his go-ahead for House Bill 216, which in part restricts the sale of non-prescription medications containing pseudoephedrine as the sole active ingredient.

That compound is found in many over-the-counter decongestants and is used as part of a recipe to make methamphetamine.

The law effectively places such medication behind the counter, where it will be distributed on a limited basis.

The legislation also establishes reporting procedures for wholesalers and retailers, all in an effort to prevent meth "cooks" from obtaining pseudo-ephedrine in the mass quantities necessary to make their illegal product.

HB 216 co-sponsor Sen. Jeff Mullis, a Republican from Chickamauga, introduced Georgia Bureau of Investigation director

Betty Brady

Scattered clouds 44°F

by Intellicast Weather

News   ▾ (GO)

Vernon M. Keenan, who remarked in opening th e ceremony that meth is not only a problem for the user, but for the general public as well.

He pointed out that "it is estimated that for each pound of meth produced, approximately five to seven pounds of toxic waste materials are also produced."

Keenan continued with praise for Rep. Jay Neal, a Republican from LaFayette and the principal author and sponsor of the bill.

"Jay Neal not only has our thanks for his tireless work on this bill, but also for his strong support of the GBI and all law enforcement in Georgia," Keenan said.

State Rep. Jay Neal, R-LaFayette, watches as Gov. Sonny Perdue signs the meth bill into law. (Messenger photo/Ken Caruthers)

Meth problem hits close to home

Rep. Neal said the inspiration for getting this law enacted came from the problems he saw with meth abuse in Walker County in work he was doing with a local drug rehabilitation facility.

"We believe we have a well-rounded bill that's going to make a real difference in the battle against methamphetamine," he said.

Gov. Perdue said methamphetamine has been a plague on the state, particularly in Northwest Georgia.

"Meth is a serious threat to Georgia families and communities. It is a highly addictive drug that alters the chemistry of the brain and, over time, the personality of those who abuse it," the governor said.

The bill is a balanced approach to a problem that was evident, Perdue said. He said he is confident the bill will give law enforcement an effective tool in working to curb meth production and abuse.

Right direction

Northwest Georgia area sheriffs were on hand at the ceremony representing Walker, Catoosa, Whitfield, Chattooga and Murray counties.

The general feeling of law enforcement leaders is that this law, which will take effect July 1, is a step in the right direction.

Walker County Sheriff Steve Wilson said he would have preferred a stronger law, pointing to Tennessee's recent anti-meth legislation.

Tennessee now allows only licensed pharmacists to sell pseudoephedrine products, and buyers are required to fill out a purchase log giving personal information.

Chickamauga Drug Store pharmacist Phil Talley said the new legislation is "past due," pointing out that his store has already had such medications behind the counter for more than a year.

At the CVS store in LaFayette, pharmacist Chris Millican said he thinks having the product behind the counter will be an effective way to stem its use in meth production.

Millican believes the new regulations won't affect the cost of products like Sudafed.

That drug's manufacturer, Pfizer Corp., now produces Sudafed PE, a decongestant product that instead contains phenylephrine, which cannot be used to make meth. However the cost for the new product is about twice that of regular Sudafed.

Talley said he thinks the trend to have some non-prescription drugs behind the counter may lead to the creation of a third class of drugs, "where you can only buy them from a pharmacy and not a grocery or convenience store."

Balanced bill

Neal did not agree with some legislators who thought to banish pseudoephedrine to pharmacies only, saying he felt it would be too restrictive for rural areas without pharmacies.

"I fear that there will be an effort to make that happen, and I don't want to see that," Neal said.

"We feel that this is a balanced enough bill and that it will be

Betty Brady

effective," Neal continued. "Now if we find out it's not, I'm going to come back in the future and do what needs to be done. But I don't think that will be necessary."

At Tuesday's bill signing the governor indicated that the intent of the law is not to have "a huge litany of drugs behind lock and key."

"Police have been fighting this battle valiantly," Perdue said. "But law enforcement is not alone. This is also a public health, social welfare and education problem."

The governor stressed the importance of bringing all the people involved together to find new strategies for fighting meth abuse, such as events like last summer's Seeking Solutions meth summit.

Becky Vaughn, president and CEO of the Georgia Council on Substance Abuse, agrees that a balanced approach is most effective.

Restricting supply while incorporating the Meth Watch program to raise community awareness and educate the public on prevention achieves that balance, she said.

"We've seen Meth Watch work in other states and we know it can make a huge difference in Georgia," Vaughn said.

EDITORIAL LEAD 5-20-04

Epidemic Of Meth

Last week's newspaper should have convinced even the most-hardened skeptics that the proliferation of methamphetamine in Chattooga County is at an epidemic level.
Most law enforcement officers have been aware of that fact for a long time.
We wish we knew the answer to the meth problem.
The ease of which it is made, the ease in which ingredients can be bought to make it and the sheer mobility of the way it can be made lends toward a culture of methamphetamine abuse and availability.
We shutter to think at how many children in this county are exposed to the toxic fumes created when meth is made. With so many people making it in their homes, it lends itself to health hazards barely comprehended today.
Even adults may be facing a future of medical problems because of the fumes.
The help for citizens who are addicted to meth is there and we hope that more meth users will see the light and decide to kick this a dangerous addiction before it is too late.
Law enforcement must continue to be ever-vigilant to those who decide they will thumb their nose at the law and make the illegal and deadly drug.
An epidemic can only be addressed by a concentrated effort by all people.

The Summerville News

The Official Legal Organ of Chattooga County, Georgia

EDITORIAL LEAD 5-20-04

Epidemic Of Meth

Last week's newspaper should have convinced even the most-hardened skeptics that the proliferation of methamphetamine in Chattooga County is at an epidemic level.
Most law enforcement officers have been aware of that fact for a long time.
We wish we knew the answer to the meth problem.
The ease of which it is made, the ease in which ingredients can be bought to make it and the sheer mobility of the way it can be made lends toward a culture of methamphetamine abuse and availability.
We shutter to think at how many children in this county are exposed to the toxic fumes created when meth is made. With so many people making it in their homes, it lends itself to health hazards barely comprehended today.
Even adults may be facing a future of medical problems because of the fumes.
The help for citizens who are addicted to meth is there and we hope that more meth users will see the light and decide to kick this a dangerous addiction before it is too late.
Law enforcement must continue to be ever-vigilant to those who decide they will thumb their nose at the law and make the illegal and deadly drug.
An epidemic can only be addressed by a concentrated effort by all people.

The Summerville News

The Official Legal Organ of Chattooga County, Georgia

JUN-06-2005 MON 03:11 PM GOVERNORS OFFICE   FAX NO. 404 463 5260   P. 03

THE STATE OF GEORGIA

EXECUTIVE ORDER

BY THE GOVERNOR:

ORDERED: That the Honorable Betty S. Brady of CHATTOOGA County, Georgia, be and is hereby appointed to serve as a member on the Georgia Commission on Women, to serve a term of office ending July 1, 2006, to succeed the Honorable Dixie S. Mooney, who resigned.

The Honorable Betty S. Brady
PO Box 291
Summerville, GA 30747

This sixth day of June, 2005.

Georgia Commission on Women

Betty S. Brady,   **Summerville, GA, Member** - Brady serves as owner and qualifying broker of Brady Realty. Prior to this, she received the Graduate Realtor Institute designation, making her the first board-designated realtor in Chattooga County. Brady is the Chairwoman and Co-Founder of the Chattooga County Citizen's Meth Task Force, a group she started with the guidance of local law enforcement to combat the use of methamphetamines in her community through education, prevention, treatment, and enforcement. She attended the business school at Walker Tech and attended Dalton College. Brady and her husband, Terrell, have two children.

Tuesday, June 07, 2005 America Online: BBrady1053

Sonny Perdue
Governor

The Summerville News,
Thursday, November 24, 2005   3-B

Brady Attends Commission On Women Meeting Nov. 16

The Georgia Commission on Women met Wednesday, Nov. 16 from 10 a.m. to 1:30 p.m. in the Senate Mezzanine Room at the State Capitol. Commissioner Betty Brady, from Chattooga, was in attendance and was accompanied to the capitol by Kaye Thomas, a local business woman.

Following the call to order, welcome, and minutes, Ms. Brady introduced her special guest, Investigator Jesse Hambrick, from Douglasville. Inv. Hambrick outlined for the group the state-wide methamphetamine problems, as well as detailing the current ephedrine laws. He presented statistics on meth, ice, crank, etc. for recent years as compared to now.

Inv. Hambrick also gave his opinion as to how the laws should be strengthened for better control. He suggested that all products containing ephedrine should be available only with a prescription.

Further, Inv. Hambrick stressed the need for drug courts and he praised citizen involvement as one of the most important factors in the drug fight.

Inv. Hambrick was invited to be on the steering committee of next year's 2006 Georgia Women's Health and Safety Expo scheduled to be held at Douglasville and is expected to address the meth and general drug problems facing Georgia.

The commission also heard from a representative of Equal Rights Amendment which is striving to ratify this amendment in Georgia.

Supreme Court Justice Harold Melton visited with the group, as did a representative of the Attorney General's office.

Letters To The Editor

Meth And Death

Editor,

Residents need to look in the mirror and take a close look into both eyes. If you are a user of Meth, see what it is doing.

There's now help to show you how you may beat the habit. Talk with Jennifer Brady.

If you were stoned out of your mind, do you even remember what you did or where doing? I think not. It burst vessels in your brain.

Go to programs offered in Summerville who want to help you. Life can be beautiful through clear eyes when your off from that junks.

Mary Childers
Summerville

The Summerville News

The Official Legal Organ of Chattooga County, Georgia

Section Three

After The Storm

What we have witnessed since Jennifer's recovery has been simply astounding. Seeing the community and state rally against the killer drug is so encouraging. The fight for good is evidenced in the the whole northwest corner of Georgia, with every county to some extent stepping up to the plate against meth.

Working together, we are attempting to get drug court in effect here. Money, of course, is the delaying factor, and the biggest obstacle we are currently delaying with. Walker, Catoosa, Dade and Chattooga Counties make up the Lookout Mountain Judicial Circuit, and we certainly want to help rehabilitate our people. Drug court is proving to be the best and most responsible way to do this.

Recent statistics released by the Georgia Department of Corrections show our county being number one in the state for meth incarcerations per capita. These stats run from 1999 thru 2004. This does not reflect or include stats since pseudo-ephedrine sales were restricted by state law in July of this year. This was mostly Mom and Pop clandestine lab statistics, and certainly it was only a fraction of what was actually being cooked.

It's encouraging to be able to say our citizen's effort is spreading. Jennifer and I have gone together to Dade County, and Whitfield County gatherings to help educate and assist in various efforts. Most of our Chattooga entourage, including the Sheriff, county commissioner and state court judge, visited Walker County to help their citizen effort's start up. Catoosa County, with my new friend, Vaneta Hullander, at the helm, seems to have a natural flow. Vaneta is a very efficient and multi - talented lady with a lot of connections. She sincerely cares about people, too.

Most of us were just average citizen's who were reeling from the shock of being 'broad - sided' by meth. We joined together and sought ways to fight back. We put our heads together, just like Douglas County Investigator Jesse Hambrick taught us. We shared ideas and initiated strategy. We studied what has already happened in places like Oklahoma and Missouri. We looked closely at our own developing trends. We knew we were definitely in the 'hot spot' , with arguably 80% of all meth cooked in the USA being within a 100 mile radius of us. It was time for action. It was much more than just a police problem. Every parent, grandparent, educator, law enforcement, emergency, and human resources worker, dealt with this. Not to mention the dangers of meeting these people on the open roads, or breathing chemical odors from neighbor's clandestine labs. Calling it an epidemic was certainly no exaggeration.

Since the new laws took effect in July '05, along with the subsequent tightening of restrictions, which were obeyed by most of our honest merchants, we are happy to report there has been an almost total cessation of active meth lab busts. This doesn't mean the meth problem has lessened. It means they have to find other avenues to produce it, and these folks are creative enough to do just that. They have developed new ways to 'cook' though the product is different and takes much longer to prepare. Then, too, we have the imported 'Ice' coming mostly from south of the border. The 'Super Labs' are a big problem, too. Thankfully, our DEA seems to be taking a firm and very present stand against this scourge.

The best news we can smile about comes from the knowledge that we successfully dealt with the clandestine labs, putting them into virtual non-existence in Georgia. This means our most precious resource, our children, aren't having to inhale the fumes anymore. This is a working wonder in itself, and a big 'laud' to our efforts. God bless everyone who played a part in this accomplishment..

As more time passes, we hear from more and more people who've recovered. Many call or come by to tell us their stories. One man, in particular, has personally shared very much with me. He is currently in his second round of major incarceration, (as we go to press). He wrote many love poems to his wife during the first stint. After his release, he did fine for awhile .... before caving in to the pressure and lure. It put him right back in the slammer.

Several of his poems are included here, with his full permission. As I read them, I get the sense of a man with time on his hands and mournful thoughts bearing on his heart. The author tells me he is truly through with it. He's lost everything except the woman he loves. He tells me their love is what will bring them through and they will make a fresh start upon his release. I pray each and every day that this will truly be the case. I know he can do it, if his heart is ready. I can sense his loneliness, so obvious through his words. He poured his heart out, leaving no doubt about his undying love for Rita, his wife. I can only wonder how meth became the focal point of his life and at what point it actually became more important than everything he held precious. It was strong enough to cause him to jeopardize all that he loved. The saying 'Meth makes you hate the ones you love, and love the ones you hate' comes to mind here.

I truly hope that all will be clearer to him when he is free again. I hope his priorities are such that he definitely can say 'no' to the devil drug methamphetamine. It will be a test of spiritual strength for him, and a big effort on his wife's part, too. Keeping temptation away means steering clear of all who engage in this activity. Old druggie buddies will have to go, if he is to have a prayer toward recovery.

Here is his heartfelt poetry, his 'reflections' of the long road he finds himself on now.

Long Walk

It's a cruel world where I've been.
But, I'm to blame for the mess I'm in.
If it was just me, it wouldn't be so bad,
But I've hurt my family, and that's what's sad.
I know they love me and God does, too.
But, I'm responsible for what I do,
I've asked God to forgive me for my sins,
And I know He will cause He's my friend.
That's one thing I knew all along,
If it weren't for Him, I'd be long gone.
I don't know why He spared me.
I guess He has a plan that I can't see.
Yes, He carried me down every road.
And when it was bad, He would carry my load.
When He walks with me, He's at his best.
He's been there before, and I've put Him through the test.
I've put Him through as many tests as He has me
But He hung right in there, and that's plain to see.
I'm sure proud that He never had my doubts,
Cause I'm walking with Him from here on out.

Frankie Watkins

Fast Lane

These wheels of justice turn very slow.
I've been here for eight months, so 1 should know.
When I get out. I'll do what's right.
And the laws I will obey,
I'll make the change and avoid *my* sinful ways.
I was living in the fast lane before I came here,
Now, my eyes are open, and 1 see very clear.
It's a dangerous life that I've lived in,
And it won't be long before I'm back out there again.
Sometimes it's hard just to do the right things,
And you never really know when it's just a game.
I've played them before and they're hard to win,
And if you lose, it may be your life's end.
Well, I got caught and thought I was through,
Then God stepped in and showed me what to do.
He put me in jail so that I could see
What it was like just to be free.
So, listen, friend, what I tell you is true,
Just do as I say, not as I do.
If life gets too hard and you lose your way,
Just remember that God's still with you every day.

Frankie Watkins

Help Me

I've been going through life sinning each day.
I ask for help. I knew no other way.
What I was doing was out of control
But what should I do? I didn't know.
Arrested and sent to jail to pay for my crimes,
I did what I did, so I stay and do my time.
I realize now that I'm alone after all.
If someone can hear me, please give me a call.
The way I was going, I knew it wouldn't last,
But it's behind *me* now, and in my past.
So I have placed my burdens at your feet,
I've put my request in your hand.
I've put my trust in your word.
When I get out, I'll be a new man.
I've been in here eight months now,
And to start my new life, I won't know how.
So, Rita, I'm depending on you,
To take me by the hand and help lead me through.
I feel so scared and all alone,
And I know I can't make it on my own.

Frankie Watkins

Missing You

Soon I'll be leaving here, my life I'll take control.
I know God has helped me, cleansed my heart and soul.
He forgave me for my sins that have grieved my heart,
helped me to be true, and gave me a chance for a new start.
Right now, it's hard for me to make any plans,
Cause there's so much out there that I don't understand.
I don't know if you're ever coming back to me,
So I pray at night and ask God "Help me, please"
I cry at night before sleep, because 1 miss you so much.
Sometimes I wake up at night, because I think I feel your touch.
If our love was a mistake, it was worth making,
And when I come home, that's the path I'll be taking.
I look back and wonder where all the years have gone,
Then I think about you and know I can't make it on my own.
Please forgive me if it's selfish to want you for my own.
Without you, I'm nothing, just a lonely man without a home.

Frankie Watkins

My Angel

Let me tell you One thing that I'd like to do.
It would be to sit down right beside you.
With my arms around you so snug and tight.
I could sit this way. night after night
My love for you, it grows and grows.
How much I love you, God only knows.
So, when you are sad and feeling blue,
Just remember, Rita, that I love you.
You fill my heart with joy and love.
You are my angel, sent from above.
Rita, you're special... .one of a kind,
and I'd like to tell the world that you are mine.
Yes, you're my angel, sent from above,
You're my sweetheart, the one I love.
Even though you have no halo or wings,
Just give, me your love and see what it brings.
Even though I'm in jail and we're far apart,
You will forever be in my heart.
I can't hug you right now, or hold you tight,
But you're in my heart, every day and night
You're in my heart, and there to stay.
I really' love you in every way.
September 13th I should be free.
Then we'll be hand in hand, just you and me.

Frankie Watkins

My Best Friend

I'm just sitting around with plenty of time,
So it's easy for me to make things rhyme.
I'm writing this poem instead of a letter,
And hope when you read it, it makes you feel better.
I may not see the path ahead, or find my way with ease,

So take me by the hand and help me, please.

It seems like I have come to my journey's end,

And I don't want to go back where I've been.

There's not many things that I haven't done.

I just lived my life and tried to have fun.

Now I have a new life just waiting for me,

But just sitting here, it's far too dim to see.

I sit here and listen to these guy's stories,

And it makes me thankful, because I have less worries.

Some of them will never be free,

And I thank God that it's not me.

I've met a lot of friends along my way,

And the sweetest of all came to see me today.

It made me so happy just to see her smile,

Came I've been away and hadn't seen her in a while.

Her name is Rita and she's my girl.

She's my best friend in the whole wide world.

I wrote her this poem today when she left this place,

And I hope when she reads it, it puts a smile on her face.

Frankie Watkins

My Life

The people I've dealt with were very strong,
And the life I've lived was very wrong.
But if I lie about my sins,
Then I'm fighting a battle I cannot win.
I keep my eyes bright and clear,
And always pay attention to what I hear
My life was so busy, and I was always stressed,
I never slowed down and got enough rest.
I did some things that got out of hand,
But if I was right, I would make a stand.
And if I was wrong, 1 would confess,
Either way, I did my best.
I'm writing these poems day by day,
About how my life has been along the way.
It's my story and I know that it's true,
So please forgive me if 1 have hurt you.

Frankie Watkins

My Little Friend

Sitting around with plenty of time,
Nothing to do and things on my mind.
Thinking about a friend of mine,
Her name is Rita, and she's very kind.
She's the sweetest girl I've ever known,
And I would like to have her for my own.
It will be a little while before I leave here,
But I'll go pick her up, if she don't care.
I'll pick her up and take her home with me,
And I'll make her happy, she will see.
She's the best friend I've ever had,
Because she makes me smile when I am sad.
It's a very hard life that she has to live,
But she's a good person with love to give.
She's my best friend and she's my girl,
And I thank God for her being in my world.

Frankie Watkins

Not Alone

I may be in jail or captivity,
But there's one thing for sure, I'll soon be free.
I'm living my life right now in despair,
So I asked for God's help. It's always there.
Whether I'm in Cedar Bluff or Washington. D.C.
There's one thing that's plain to see.
He's been with me every day in here.
Sometimes I think He's the only one who cares.
Why I stayed here, I was concerned ..
But God kept me here so I could learn.
It was the simple things in life that I couldn't see,
And they were the ones that meant the most to me.
I lost the things that mattered the most,
It was *my* fault that I lost what I lost.
When I leave here, I'll be a better man,
And I won't make the same mistakes over again.

Frankie Watkins

Rehabilitated

I screwed up my life and they sent me to jail,
They wouldn't give me a bond or set me no bail,
They sent me to rehab to rehabilitate,
And I did good there. I guess you can see.
They sent me all the way down to Mobile,
And I made it with ease, because it was God's will.
I thought at first I wouldn't like the place,
Because there were men there from every race
I really enjoyed being down there.
I was around people that really cared.
I sure would like to get out of this jail,
So I could call my friends down there,
And tell them I'm doing well.
I had lots of fun during my stay,
I met new people every day.
All the people there really liked *me*,
They said I was a nut,
But there was some hope that they could see.
They brought me back to jail to do 90 more days,
But I hope to leave here this coming Wednesday.

Frankie Watkins

Second Chance

My words and deeds are very small,
And what I say hardly counts at all.
A heartfelt tear will show my love,
Because the words I say never do.
It says I want to share your pain,
And my heart goes out to you.
You have always deserved so much better,
So I'm writing this poem instead of a letter.
I know you've almost slipped right through my hands,
So I will show you that I'm a better man.
I don't need no promises to make it right.
I just need you to hold me real tight.
A second chance is what I'm talking about.
I can make it right, there is no doubt
So, please hold me tight cause I am hurting.
You're the only one that can help, that's for certain.
The time I've spent alone gets very old,
And the darkness there gets very cold.
So, I will do the only thing I know to do.
I will pray for me and 1 will pray for you.

Frankie Watkins

Someone Special

I have something special for the girl I love,
A gift of never ending love.
A love that is not greedy, selfish, or untrue,
The love I have is forgiving and pure.
It makes we so happy that I want to cry,
It puts lumps in my throat and tears in my eyes. There's been sadness,
loneliness, and pain.
I knew our love was going through a change.
Listen to this poem, because it is true.
I love her so much, and she loves me, too.
Tears in my eyes from things on my mind,
Years of living in a world so unkind.
A story of love right here in my hands.
I'm searching for knowledge, I don't understand.
I need to be greater than what I am.
Should 1 walk a straight line, or not give a damn?
The secrets and answers I do not know.
I'm looking for secrets that haven't been told.
Mysteries of my heart and answers in life,
I will find in the arms of my loving wife,

Frankie Watkins

The Train

I've seen the train run many times,
And take my friends away.
It takes them down south,
And gives them new rules to follow and obey.
When I woke up this morning, there again was the train.
It came for *my* friend Fuzzy today.
For some of us, there seems to be no answers,
But we still are looking for a better way,
There's so much in here I cannot see,
For my eyesight is far too dim,
But, there's a lot of good men in here,
So I put my trust in them.
And when I'm feeling sad and sinking low,
look to my friends in here, and love and compassion flow.
It's a different world living in here.
But we're all close and really care.
We're the ones that did the crimes,
So we suffer and live in pain.
But, in the end, we'll be the ones
Who have the most to gain.
So, we stay in jail and do our time,
And hope someday to be free again.

Frankie Watkins

Thinking It Over

I've no cause now for worry or fear, Because you are gone, and that
is clear. 1 can't look back on yesterday,
Because the love I had is gone away.
It is your heart that I will set free,
So now I'm ashamed of what I see.
I'm no longer in your world, but I won't forget
The good times we had when we first met.
Sometimes it's hard just to go another day,
And accept what has happened, without delay
I'm hurting so bad from losing you,
And my life seems hopeless, but what can I do?
Life is so short, and goes so fast,
But the love I had, I thought would last.
So, when I lay down at night to sleep,
I still find it hard not to weep.
I wanted so bad Just to be with you,
But the promises you made, I see were untrue.
But just like a flower, I will live and grow,
And my love for you will surely show.

Frankie Watkins

𝒯ime 𝓜arches 𝒪n

Sitting in jail, seems my life has stopped.
All I do is count the days and watch the clock. 1 didn't have help, I
got here on my own,
So I sit and watch as time marches on.
I once had a life, but it fell apart,
So here I sit with my broken heart.
It's a broken heart that will never be mended,
Till my life is over, and has ended.
The loneliness I carried was a heavy load,
But there's nothing left now, I have no goals.
When I leave this jail, I'll be a different man,
But I'll start over somewhere if I can.
As I look back on the life I've had,
I can't understand why it went so bad.
The past few years, I was a lonely man,
But it's over now, so I can start again.

Frankie Watkins

Walk With Me

Please take me by the hand and walk with me,
And show me the love that I can't see.
You can be my friend and guide,
Please, Rita, just stay by my side.
I need you more now than 1 ever had,
If you can be with me, I wilt surely be glad.
I know I've done wrong in the past,
But our love is strong and will always last.
Please believe what I'm telling you.
Because the love I have will be true
I miss you more every day.
At visitation, I don't know what to say.
There's been so much that I wanted to do,
But nothing really seemed to matter to you.
I have never been one to give up a fight,
But I will give up to *you*, cause 1 want things to be right

Frankie Watkins

Which Way

Living with you in a life that is true,
And striving to please is all that I do
So you need to extend a loving hand,
And show me love without demand.
The love I had grew strong and true,
But I didn't know what you would do.
Now, I see the sign that our love was small.
I did *my* best to give it my all.
So right now, I'm trying to decide
If I really want you by my side.
The freedom to choose is a gift of mine,
So all I can say is it will take time.
I didn't know when you were gone
That I would feel so all alone.
It's been so bad since your depart.
It left me sad and with a broken heart.
So I ask for help from the man above
To show me a life with peace and love.

Frankie Watkins

"Another" One's Man's Story

Another 'one' man is someone Jennifer knew when she was struggling in addiction. In and out of jails, fighting demons everywhere, seeing his children follow his footsteps into addiction, incarceration, and untold misery, all have taken quite a toll on this one man.

Looking and apparently feeling much older than he actually is, he is suffering the physical effects of his self - induced mischief. He shares his story under condition of anonymity, and he sincerely hopes all users will listen and 'wise up.' He wants to help people avoid the long black train. His story is very touching, and very factual.

We certainly hope and pray he will be strong. His children and grandchildren need him, and I know his christian mother prays daily for her son and entire biological lineage.

Read his story, and please say a prayer for all of them.

One Man's Story

I use to use meth. When I first started using meth, I started selling this drug thinking I was going to make some quick money off of it. Then, one night, I went by this girl's house to see how she was doing. Until this night, I had just smoked it on foil or in a glass tube or snorted lines of it.

After I got inside her house, I went with her to the bathroom. I was really surprised to see her shooting the meth up into her veins. She asked me if I wanted to try it. I looked at her and I don't even know why but I said 'yes, give me a shot.' After that one shot, I knew I was in trouble. The next think I knew was hours had gone by and I had done another shot. Then it turned daylight, and here I was doing another.

After about a week had went by, I was still up shooting more and more meth. In between shots of meth, I would smoke some. I got to where this seemed like one of the best highs I had ever experienced. I couldn't believe I would get so tired and sleepy and all I had to do was just a little more meth and I would be wide awake and feel normal. This blowed my mind. I really never even thought about being hooked on this drug.

It got to where I liked it so much that I really started just hanging with people who cooked this stuff. I probably wasted a couple thousand dollars learning how to make the stuff. Once I started getting it to come out the way I liked it, I didn't want none from anyone else. I just wanted to do what I had made. I really felt like I was some kind of god because of the stuff I was making. Everyone that tried some of it wanted more. At this time, I never even realized that the meth I was making was even harmful to anyone.

Meth had me totally blinded that I was making a drug that was totally destroying people's lives. I started noticing that couples, as long as they were doing this dope, seemed to get along fine. But when they ran out of it, they would get into fights and fusses. This started bearing on my mind, that I was the one who was ruining people's relationships. At this time, I still wasn't paying any attention to what it was doing to my life. While I was doing this drug, I really didn't care. I had all kinds of girlfriends and guys who would call me or come and see me. I really thought that I was making something that others and myself could really enjoy.

I got to where I didn't want to get rid of any of it. I only wanted to do it with people that I was running around with. I would even trade it for sex, or would sell just enough to get the chemicals and materials to make more. People would try to trade me almost anything to get this stuff from me.

I finally realized that with as many people knowing that I cooked and kept meth, the law had to know about it, too. So, I decided I had to move to other counties to make this drug. I went to Calhoun first. Then I went to Florida. Then I went to Tulsa, Oklahoma, and on to Manhattan, New York, and the Bronx. After several years of moving here and there, I started realizing that I, myself, had developed a dependence on this stuff.

I wouldn't feel normal without doing drugs. I knew my life was going straight to hell. No one had to tell me anything. The people that really loved me tried to talk to me. This was so strange to me. I didn't give a damn about the people who loved me. The only ones that I cared about at that time were the people that wanted to do this dope with me. I didn't ever want to be around anyone unless they did this dope with me.

My son even developed a dependence on this same drug. I never asked him where he got his dope from. We would just share his dope or mine with each other. At this time, we were doing this meth together and both of us seemed to be happy. It didn't matter that we were awake for a week or even how long it was. I know, at one time, he and I were awake for 19 days.

I finally started seeing spots and would even see shadows of people who weren't even there. I finally told my son 'I'm going home and going to bed.' I knew my body system couldn't handle much more. After I went home and to bed, I slept for about three days. When I woke up, I tried to get in touch with my son. Finally, I got a call from the jail. My son had gotten busted with meth. He served two years in a detention center for this, not to mention the fines and fifteen years probation.

After this, I started hanging around with my daughter. We both were enjoying the same thing as far as shooting up meth. At this time, the 'high' seemed to be the best thing that we could be doing. I started noticing that all my daughter wanted anymore was just another shot of meth. This started to hurt me when I noticed that every time I would see her, either she would go straight to the bathroom and do her shot or she would ask me if I had any. She would even catch me asleep and would search for mine until she found it. Then she would lie to me and tell me she didn't get any from me.

At this time, I knew my daughter needed help. I started feeling like I needed help more than she did. I finally left and went to Clearwater, Florida and stayed for three months. All I did was cook dope almost everyday. When I came back from down there, my body system was worn out. I had hardly slept any the whole time I was gone.

I finally started getting on my knees and praying to God to please help me. I knew my life had gotten out of control. I really tried to stop doing meth. I even gave away all of my meth, but this didn't work. People that I had gave dope to or done dope with, whenever they could find me, would invite me to their place and I would go because of my weakness. At that time, I would do more.

I finally cooked about ten grams one night. The next day, I wanted to go home, but the person I was with wanted me to ride with him to town. I told him not to go to the Wal Mart, but he did. He went in and bought a couple of things to make meth with. I didn't go in. When we left, the law pulled us over. They carried him to jail that day. They let me go. Ten days later, they came with a warrant for criminal attempt to manufacture meth. They arrested me and carried me to jail. They gave me a thirty five thousand dollar bond.

When I got up to call someone to come and sign my bond, my probation officer came in. He asked how I was doing. I told him 'pretty good' and asked how he was doing. He said ' you don't have dirty urine, do you?' I immediately said "Yes, I do.' He said 'what do you have in your system?' I told him 'methamphetamine and marijuana.' He asked, 'Is that all ?'I said 'yes' and he told me he would tell the judge that I admitted to this. I thought this would help by admitting it instead of taking the test. They put a probation hold on me.

Well, I slept for the first two weeks that I was in jail. My body system was completely worn down. I started getting more and more depressed as the days went by. It wasn't only the part about being locked up. Really, having to do without meth after I had been using it daily for at least five years was rough. My body was starting to go through hell. I didn't weigh but 135 pounds when I normally weighed 165 to 175 pounds. All I could do was pray more and more and ask for God's help.

The law wouldn't understand what I was experiencing so I never tried to explain to no one just what I was experiencing. I kept this between me and God. Well, after three months, I went to a revocation hearing and they took all my probation. I was short two weeks doing two years for a drug test that I admitted to. They sent me to a detention center.

I kept praying to God to please remove my addiction for meth from my system. After I had been locked up for over a year, I finally started reading more and more about meth and the effects it had on your mind and what it does to your body. I was really surprised to find out that no matter how you did this drug, either snorting, eating, shooting or smoking it, meth attacks all the organs you have in your body. This was really scary for me to find out.

While I was doing this drug, no one could have gotten through to me that this drug kills you from the inside. I never thought that it caused the harm to your body organs that it does. Not to mention that it kills your brain cells to the point where you won't listen to anyone who tries to tell you what it's really doing to you.

I went back to a jury trial about six months before I was released from the detention center. They tried me under a life sentence. Thank God I was found 'not guilty.'

Right after my trial, my son had gotten out of the two year sentence he had, and he was doing good for himself. Then for some reason, he started back doing meth. Now he's incarcerated with no bond and has some serious charges on account of meth.

My daughter got detention because of her addiction. This was before I got out. She skipped court and is now doing ninety days in a woman's out-reach program. She is saying right now that she will not mess with meth anymore. I pray for her and my son everyday.

You can very easily see that meth has separated my immediate family. My son tells me he isn't going to mess with meth ever again. He asked me, ' please,dad, don't get messed up with this meth anymore.' He and I haven't been around each other except for about five times in almost four years now.

I would have never dreamed that a drug would separate either of us like this. I know there is probably no telling, within ten years, what using this drug has done to each of our insides. I know I had blood tests done while I was in the detention center and I thank God that I'm in good health. I am sure I have some brain damage and possibly other damage to my lungs because of meth.

Anyone who would just find out what meth really does to their body systems and would really pay attention to what it does to people that really love them, would probably take this meth a little more serious than just staying up day after day.

I think the devil has developed this evil drug called meth. I believe that the addiction to this drug is a epidemic. To me, as easy as the access of this drug is, this is, more than likely, one of the plagues the Bible speaks of. I really don't know anyone that has ever tried this drug and said they didn't like it at first. But I do know a lot of people that has lost everything that they ever had. I know a lot of people who really loved each other and their relationships were destroyed.

It's hard for me to even think about kids who don't live with their parents because family and children's services had to intervene. This is pretty sad, knowing that most parents, deep in their hearts, love their kids. Their addiction blinds them to their own children.

A year ago, if I had gotten out of detention, I believe I could've talked to my kids before they got in trouble. I hope and pray that God lets someone have the knowledge to find a cure to what is taking place. People are going to see people that we love die from what's going on with meth. The one's that live and use this drug for the next ten years are going to develop diseases that can be transmitted to others. Not to mention what their bodies will start looking like.

I don't know what, if anything, anyone will get out of reading this. I at least want anybody who reads this to remember this. You will either go to an asylum or to jail. If you are a lucky addict and realize this before it's too late, maybe it won't be your last choice. Meth is very sneaky. It makes you feel like nothing is wrong.

If you don't trust what I'm writing, get some literature and find out for yourself. Meth does kill. I will never cook it again in my whole life. I know myself and my conscience would not leave me alone if I kept letting people get something from me that would contribute to someone's death.

For my own health and my family being separated because of meth, this is enough for me to stop. I will continue praying not to be in contact with it again in my lifetime. Anyone who reads this really should think about themselves and their families. It hurts family members to watch loved ones slowly kill themselves. Life has more to offer than to stay up everyday and ruin your body system.

If you really love yourself, quit meth. Chemicals were not made for the human body. If you have never tried this drug, don't try it. It does kill.

Anonymous

Beauty Queen

I met this young woman one night after she called me, directly, asking for help. She'd been in a bad relationship of abuse, drugs, and all that goes along with it. All her self respect was gone. She cried over the phone, saying she wanted to change. She wanted to feel human again. She wanted to be off meth. She wanted to be a mother to her two precious children again. The children lived with her parents, and her maternal heart strings were pulling at her. She was a mess, and she was asking for our help.

I went to see her personally that night. I might add, this was against all the rules, and everyone's better judgement. In this respect, *everyone* means our law enforcement advisors and combined voices of wisdom on the task force. Normally, calls were made directly to our hotline and from there were delegated to proper authorities. But, she had called me directly and asked for help. I felt the sincerity of her plea. The thought I could not ignore was 'she's someone's daughter.' Someone probably had helped my daughter when she was in the same condition. I had to go. That's all there was to it. So, I said a prayer and went.

I wound up taking her to our local Sheriff's Department to meet with one of our best and most trusted officers. He talked with her, and I can truly add, with tremendous compassion in his voice. Then he arranged for her to go into a shelter and even authorized transport. Our collective prayers were strong for this young woman.

Sadly, she struggled with staying at the shelter. It seems she might've convinced herself that she'd do better outside, in the real world. It was too soon to leave, and before long, we heard she was back with the same guy. All the old misery was repeating itself.

This was quite sad, and we all felt the sting of failure. However, (and this is something we're seeing more and more), this young woman resurfaced several months later. She'd found new strength and it helped her to start over. She got a job and is currently applying herself diligently toward getting her life back. She wants to do right by her children, her parents, and herself. God be with her.

Her story re-emphasizes how hard it is to 'stay quit.' It's so easy to just give in, to go back to the self - defeating life style of drug addiction.

Many prayers have been said for this young woman. I believe she is another recovery 'miracle' in the works. I believe God has plans for her.

My Conclusions

We could go on and on with more stories like these, but for the sake of space and time, we will summarize by saying we believe that each battle and recovery can and must be fought individually. No one plan, other than accepting God's will and trusting Him completely, can bring recovery to all addicts.

We've found that people respond and react differently. Those with strong family support have the highest success rates. Others seem to be more alone, and theirs is truly the 'rough row to hoe.'

I wish I could truly describe how it feels to accidentally meet up with one of these guys or girls in recovery and know they are still doing well and getting their act together. So what if they had to start over. They're definitely more mature and they know about endurance.

One young woman described it as having to learn everything all over again. I can only imagine the difficulty. I can say I am very thankful and appreciative for all the citizen 'warriors' who rally to help these poor souls. The Vaneta Hullanders, Clint Young's, Toni Busbin's, Jesse Hambrick Jr's, Son Rise Ministries, Steve Box's, just to name a few, are all angels in my opinion. All fighting the good fight, trying to lead God's wayward children back to recovery and hopefully, the fold.

Isn't this what we're supposed to do? Isn't this what God expects of us ? We all have our troubles, trials, personal tragedies and hardships to bear. I deeply respect any and all the good people who can lay their 'self' aside and reach out to help others. There's so many ways to pitch in and help. One well-to-do man tells me that people hate him so he can't be visible in our effort. Still, he can and does donate monetarily. This effort can always use money.

Another tells me she loves manning the hotline -- it gives her such a sense of helping people. She loves being part of the effort. It's interesting that she's disabled, with only part of her heart working. It has got to be the 'big' part of her heart that drives her on. She handed out candy and 'drug free' brochures at our Halloween Candy Walk and she enjoyed herself as much or more than any of the kids did.

There is a job, or vital service, that can be performed by almost everyone who truly wants to help. Sometimes just listening and offering a caring hand of friendship to a down trodden person is priceless to them.

Some of us did public service announcements which played for months on local radio. Others visited neighboring counties to provide support and assistance. Dedication was, and still is, our big driving force. We believe in what we're doing. It's a big plus when news media outlets help spread awareness by giving good press to our efforts.

We know meth won't go away overnight. There's simply too much money and power involved. Corrupt people love power and money. It doesn't matter what they have to do or how many people get hurt or destroyed. All they want is what they want. It is their driving force. They are evil and dangerous. They lack respect for human life, and they have no conscience. Innocent blood is on their hands.

Still, our God is not willing for any of us to perish. He wants all of us to come home. What I have come to realize is that it's easier for the user to give it up than for the supplier to stop. This vile love of money and power is despicable. I hope they all stop before it's too late for their souls. The Bible says it's a terrible thing to fall into the hands of the living God. I wholeheartedly believe this.

I'd like to mention a very special friend I've come to know thru this effort. I met him in church, and he instantly got my attention. I was very impressed with his insightfulness and intense love for God's children. He has contacted me several times, bringing messages especially for me, from God. He expresses it this way, and I believe him. He is on the inside track of prophecy, and everything he's said has been accurate so far. He tells me who to avoid, and who to be careful of. He tells me who runs to the bad guys with information, hoping to sabotage our efforts. He's also given me assurances of the presence of strong angels. He tells me who the angels are protecting. He also told (and I shook with fear and humbleness) of how I now have the blood of Jesus on me because of all our efforts to help people. It makes me feel very humble, and it makes me want to carry on. It makes me want to say to the Lord, 'show me where you want me to go, use me if I can be used, and make me a worthy tool, an obedient child of the King.' This is my daily prayer. I trust in the Lord to make things right. I know He will deliver.

And I'm happy to report that Jennifer's prayers have been answered about seeing her step-daughter again. The child's father has actually brought her to visit. It was a joyous and tearful reunion. We all love her dearly. We always will. She knows it and so do we.

Jennifer is growing intellectually, too. She's becoming very self-sufficient. She's holding down a good job - for this area. She owns her own home and this has done wonders for her peace of mind. She's still single and personally I hope she stays that way for a long time. At least until she is very ready to commit her heart. I pray that God will lead her to a loving and healthy relationship with a mature, responsible Christian man who will treasure her and love her dearly. This can only happen when the time is right, and I keep praying she will be patient and wait for the right one.

As for me, I am still pursuing new goals, as well as working everyday. New doors are opening, new opportunities are on the horizon. I know there is a master plan at work here, and I'm humbled and honored to be included in it. God is good.

We will continue being part of this effort. We will willingly serve. Again, I'd like to say that I am very thankful for all the good people who have risen to the meth challenge. All these warriors are doing a tremendous service for their fellow man and woman. Surely, our just and loving God will reward these efforts accordingly.

About the Author

Betty Brady lives in Summerville, GA. with her family. This is her first book. It was written because she understands the pain, heartbreak, and fear that comes with addiction, as well as the shame that prevents many families from seeking help. Written to inspire hope, this book is straight from the heart.

Printed in the United States
98872LV00004B/445/A